MICROMAN

Microman

What Life Might Be Like
if You Were Bill Gates

I.B. McIntosh

ARSENAL PULP PRESS
Vancouver

ARSENAL PULP PRESS
103 · 1014 Homer Street
Vancouver B.C.
Canada V6B 2W9
www.arsenalpulp.com

This book is a work of satire for entertainment purposes only.
It has not been reviewed, approved or endorsed by Bill
Gates or the Microsoft Corporation.

Every effort has been made to obtain permission for quoted
material. If there has been an omission or error, the author and
the publisher would be grateful to be informed.

Printed and bound in Canada by Webcom Ltd.

Cover design by Russ Bugera
Cover photo by Chris Relke, *Vancouver Province*
Text design by Huge Grant

CANADIAN CATALOGUING IN PUBLICATION DATA:

McIntosh, I.B., 1969-
Microman

Includes bibliographical references.

ISBN 1-55152-057-5

1. Gates, Bill, 1955- Humour. I. Title.
HD9696.C62G3356 1998   338.7'610053'092   C98-910434-6

The 50 Billion Dollar Question

At some point in our lives every one of us has looked around the room or across the table at our friends and family and asked the question: "What would you do if you had a million dollars?"

"Buy a new house."

"Send my parents on a trip around the world."

"Send my kids to Harvard or Yale or Princeton."

"Buy a car, take a vacation."

"Buy the [insert professional sports team here]."

Well, these days a loaf of bread costs more than a dime, cars aren't getting any cheaper, and the size of the richest fortunes is increasing. The question had to change.

Now the question is: What would you do if you had fifty billion dollars?

For starters, you'd be Bill Gates.

He's the richest man in the world and although some people claim that his net worth, which comes from the value of his Microsoft stock, is tenuous (in its 1997 400 Richest list, *Forbes* claimed that "in a volatile market Gates' net worth can gain or drop a billion bucks on a tremor"), he's still worth more than fifty billion dollars. In fact, in its 1998 list *Forbes* ranked Gates top in the world with fifty-one billion dollars and as of July 1, 1998, his net worth was over fifty-six billion dollars.

One of the challenges of presenting history is its inability to be captured by a single interpretation.

$50,000,000,000.00.

What would you do if you had that much money at your disposal?

What might your life be like if you were Bill Gates?

In the early eighties, Bill Gates was a relative unknown. Just an average guy trying to make a living. But when Microsoft stock was first offered to the public, Bill Gates became an instant celebrity: his stock in the company, literally overnight, was suddenly worth $306 million. He hit the pages of *U.S. News & World Report* on July 21, 1986, at age thirty, as the fifty-sixth richest American, the youngest on the list of one hundred. The 1986 *Forbes 400* had Gates placed in the "$200 million or more" category with a net worth estimated at $315 million. *Forbes* editors then described Gates as a "true believer in the computer crusade."

I think it's unusual that someone can have so much money.

Since then, as Microsoft's presence and influence have risen – presiding over the world-wide technological revolution – so has Bill's profile, to the point where he has been on the covers of such prestigious magazines as *Time* and *Newsweek*. He was awarded the Price Waterhouse Leadership Award for Lifetime

Achievement in 1993. He was thirty-eight.

Barbara Walters interviewed him. He was lampooned on *The Simpsons*. There is international interest in where he lives, how he spent his honeymoon, what kind of art he buys.

What would you say in an interview?

Who would you give money to?

Where would you go?

What would you do with your fifty billion dollars?

What would your life be like if you were Bill Gates?

Reality can be subjective.

There are elements of truth in all mythology.

Microman in the
eighth grade.

Author's Note

To Aspiring Micromen and Microwomen of the World

I can't speak for anyone else, but I'm jealous. Envious. I'd like to know what it's like to be so rich, so admired, to have so much influence on the world, to be dearly loved and venomously hated. I'd like to know what it's like to be Bill Gates, Microman.

And I've been watching. Closely. Watching the numbers rise, the dialogue build, his image shift. Putting together the pieces, trying to construct a picture of the life of a Microman. How did Microman get his start? What were his lucky breaks? When Microman gets hungry, where does he eat? Who is he and who does he want to be? Why?

I'd like to be a chief executive officer. A chairman. I'd like to have a house built to accommodate my every whim and desire. I'd like to drive fast cars at breakneck speeds and spend millions on a single piece of art-

Information at your fingertips.

– Microsoft motto

work. I'd like to have people – politicians and conventioneers especially – climbing over each other to be seen with me. I'd like to have access to anything I want – however capricious – anytime I want it. I'm intrigued at the idea of having, at my disposal, a team of public relations staff. Who do I want to be today?

The best I can do right now is be president of the International Society of Micromen and Women. Society members – men and women from around the world – have dedicated themselves to attaining the stature of Micromen. While opinions of Gates and Microsoft vary, Micromen and Microwomen are determined to become as rich and powerful as he is.

Microman: What Life Might Be Like If You Were Bill Gates is the primer, the handbook, the guide to achieving this lofty goal. In these pages are hints and tips at becoming Micromen, answers to the questions we all have about the life of the man who may be poised to quite literally take over the world.

Photographs, data, and anecdotes all help to develop a profile of the penultimate Microman. While all statistics, unless otherwise noted, are as of July 1, 1998, keep in mind that Bill's net worth, and the status of his company, Microsoft, change daily. To help you stay up-to-date, all sources of information are listed at the end of the book. Keep an eye peeled.

Spread the word. The success of the International Society of Micromen and Women depends on the support of its members. Tell your friends and family how easy it can be to live like Microman. Together we can build an organization that can make billions and wield power over the world.

Then maybe Bill will come to one of our meetings.

Microman at age 3½
with mom, Mary.

Microbasics

Who Are You?

In Seattle, Washington, at just after 9 p.m. on October 28, 1955, you were born. Your parents gave you the name William Henry Gates, a name you share with your father and grandfather. You are Bill Gates III.

You grew up privileged, compared to most Americans. Your father was a lawyer and your mother sat on the boards of banks, universities, and charities. You never worried about where your next meal was coming from. You were likely somewhat sheltered from the harsher realities of life given that you grew up in the suburbs of Seattle. You didn't walk past inner-city slums everyday. You were never confronted by armed soldiers on your front lawn.

As a child you were precocious, reportedly signing your sister to an agreement that, for five dollars, allowed you unrestricted access to her baseball mitt. And you did things your own way, in your own time. Although your parents encouraged good grades by

Some people are bound to get better information technology than others, just as some inevitably have better access to food, shelter, transportation, medical care, education, and entertainment.

offering a quarter for every "A," you had to decide for yourself that you wanted straight "As." In one summer your grade point average went from 2.2 to 4.

That determination also showed in your attempt, when you were eight, to read through the *World Book Encyclopedia*. In five years you had reached the Ps. By that time, another interest had come into your life and the encyclopedia got suddenly boring.

You were – are – strong-willed. You argued with and defied your mother and school was not the best place for you. In the sixth grade, your parents thought it would be best to send you to talk with a professional. Later you remember the child psychiatrist you visited as being just like the one from *Ordinary People*. He gave you books to read and got you thinking "a little differently."

In grade seven, your parents decided to take you out of public school. They were worried about how you might fit in because your "interests were so very different from the typical sixth grader's." Instead you attended Lakeside School, a private institution that has been described as "elite" and "advanced."

I was fortunate enough to be raised in a family that encouraged kids to ask questions.

Trey didn't have a lot of confidence in social settings.
– *your father*

Fear should guide you, but it should be latent.

VITAL STATISTICS

NAME
William Henry Gates III

KNOWN ALIASES
Trey

DATE OF BIRTH
October 28, 1955, approx. 9 p.m.

ASTROLOGICAL SIGN
Scorpio

HEIGHT
average

WEIGHT
average

HANDEDNESS
ambidextrous

PARENTS
William Gates Junior, lawyer; Mary Gates (nee Maxwell), teacher, regent, board member

Microbasics Microjobs Microvisits Microvehicles Microhome
Microplay Microriches Micropolitics Microgiving Microfolk
Microreligion Microworries Microdreams Microimage Microman

17

At Lakeside you started to grow into yourself. You were in a school play and it was at Lakeside that you saw – and played with – your first computer. You wrote programs that played Tic-Tac-Toe and Risk.

It was also where you met – and became friends with – Paul Allen, who later became your partner in the formation of Microsoft.

In 1973, you entered Harvard to study applied mathematics, although at times you considered economics and law. You didn't really bother with computer science. You knew more than the professors, you were cocky in conversations with computer science graduate students when pointing out problems with their thinking, and the thought of having to sit in a classroom staring at code on a blackboard bored you to tears. You wanted to be doing stuff.

In 1974, in a story that has become legend, Paul Allen came running into your dorm room waving a magazine in the air. On the cover of that issue of *Popular Electronics* was a picture of the first personal computer, The Altair. Legend has it that Paul yelled out to you: "It's happening. And we're going to miss it!"

SIBLINGS
Kristi, born 1954
Libby, born 1964

OCCUPATION
Chief Executive Officer & Chairman, Microsoft Corporation

MARITAL STATUS
Married, January 1, 1994 to Melinda Gates (nee French)

CHILDREN
one, Jennifer Katharine, born April 26, 1996

ADDRESS
somewhere on the shore of Lake Washington, in Medina (Seattle)

PHONE
not available

EMAIL
askbill@ microsoft.com

We became concerned about him. . . . He was so small and shy, in need of protection, and his interests were so very different.

– your father, on your entering junior high school

I felt that I understood computers well enough, that I really didn't need to hang out with a computer crowd [at Harvard].

It's like walking the Vatican with the Pope.
– *Tom Brokaw, after walking through Comdex 1995 with you*

In your junior year, 1975, you took a leave of absence from Harvard and moved to Albuquerque, New Mexico, with Paul. You weren't about to be left behind. The information age was creeping into the world, just as you had imagined, and this was too good a chance to pass up. The small programming company that you established in the SouthWestern desert – Micro-Soft, later renamed Microsoft – was formed. History turned a corner.

The most valuable thing to you is your time. You'd gamble, you say, if the payoff was not money, but time. You are ambidextrous, able to use either hand equally well, and your tendency to rock back and forth when you are thinking – processing information – has become the characteristic most copied by your admiring fans.

Just because someone with a calculator recently deemed me the richest businessman in the world doesn't mean I'm a genius.
(July 18, 1995)

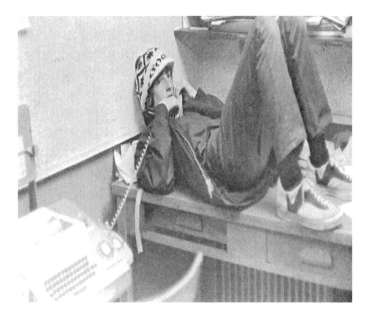

Microbasics Microjobs Microvisits Microvehicles Microhome
Microplay Microriches Micropolitics Microgiving Microfolk
Microreligion Microworries Microdreams Microimage Microman

19

MICROMAN COMPARED TO AUTISTICS

YOU	AUTISTICS
[You are] just smarter than everyone else. – Microsoft executive Mike Maples	Some autistics possess an "excellent ability of logical abstract thinking.
People who know [you] know that you have to bring him into a group ... because he doesn't have the social skills to do it on his own. – *former girlfriend*	Autistics suffer "impairment of social interaction with others."
"While [you] are working, [you] rock.... [Your] upper body rocks down to an almost forty-five degree angle, rocks back up, rocks down again."	Many autistics show "repetitive or automatic movements, such as spasms, tics, rocking." Some autistic children "rock back and forth."
"If [you] strongly disagrees with what [someone is] saying, [you are] in the habit of blurting out, 'That's the stupidest fucking thing I've ever heard!' People tell stories of [you] spraying saliva into the face of some hapless employee."	Autistic children sometimes suffer "sudden panics or rages, and scream or hit out uncontrollably."
"[You] did not look at [the reporter] very often but either looked down as [you were] talking or lifted [your] eyes above [the reporter's] head to look out the window."	Autistics "do not make eye contact."
"[You have] planned a full-size trampoline for the house [you are] building."	The home of one autistic family had a "well-used trampoline, where the whole family, at times, likes to jump and flap their arms."

They claim I started at an extremely young age. *(on your inclination to rock back and forth)*

source: New Yorker, *December 27, 1996, January 3, 1997,*
quoted in Why Bill Gates is Richer Than You, *Philip Greenspun.*

Microman and
Paul Allen, July 1981.

Microjobs

Bringing Home the Bacon

LAKESIDE PREPARATORY SCHOOL

If you were Bill Gates, the first software program you wrote played Tic-Tac-Toe. The Mothers' Club at Lakeside School had purchased a computer terminal for students with proceeds from a rummage sale. From the moment you laid eyes on that terminal, you were hooked. It got to the point where you were sneaking out of your bedroom late at night, not to raise hell in the neighborhood, but to access cheap, late-night computer time.

Because the computer at the school was simply a terminal, and whoever used it had to pay for processing time, you needed money. You had to scrounge up enough cash to pay for your computer-time-fix. Your parents had instilled the values that kept you from becoming a thief, and a paper route must have

I've lived my life thinking about software.

The problems of America's schools are not insurmountable, just extremely complicated.

Teachers were fairly dignified in those days and usually were supposed to know what was going on. *(on why students at Lakeside School monopolized the computer terminal)*

The teachers thought we were quite unusual.

I'd skip out on athletics and go down to this computer center [near the University of Washington].

A leader needs both vision and the ability to communicate it.

seemed mundane, so you offered your services as a tester to local computer companies. In exchange for finding problems – bugs – in their software, you were paid in computer time.

Then you got a job programming. You formed the Lakeside Programmers Group with Paul Allen, Ric Weiland, and Kent Evans. Kent, who was your age and your best friend, died tragically when the two of you were in the eleventh grade. A company in Portland, Oregon hired the Lakeside Programmers Group to design and write a payroll program. When the group wasn't sure there was enough work to go around, you were kicked out. But the deadline was fast approaching, and they needed you. You agreed to come back under the condition that you got to be in charge. That was all it took.

That business deal was followed by a job for Lakeside School, who paid the group $2,400 to write a program to arrange class schedules for students. While you have been a computer nerd from early on, and you only had eyes for that first love, the notion of the opposite sex was creeping into your life: you programmed the scheduler to place you in classes filled with girls.

In 1972, a young electronics company named Intel released their first microprocessor that industry insiders believed would help establish terminals, but which you and Paul knew could be programmed. You and Paul had been watching the computer industry closely, and predicted that microprocessors, computer brains, would become more powerful and much smaller, ultimately functioning as well as minicomputers.

Microbasics **Microjobs** Microvisits Microvehicles Microhome
Microplay Microriches Micropolitics Microgiving Microfolk
Microreligion Microworries Microdreams Microimage Microman

23

Perhaps as a result of Kent's death your friendship with Paul became stronger. Paul left Seattle for Pullman, Washington to attend university. You kept in touch, often taking the bus to visit him and writing code for another software program to work on the new Intel chip. The Traf-O-Data machine was designed to analyze traffic information compiled by traffic counting machines. While companies paid you to analyze their data, no company would buy the machine from a couple of kids. It didn't matter, though. You and Paul had your first taste of true entrepreneurship. You liked it.

But before you could make your move you had to exercise patience, waiting for a manufacturer to produce a more powerful chip. Intel obliged in 1974, releasing a chip with ten times the power of the chip that ran Traf-O-Data. By this time you had moved to Cambridge, Massachusetts to attend Harvard. This time Paul followed you.

I'm extremely careful about what I promise employees, and I don't overuse praise because I want my compliments to be genuine and meaningful.

I don't think there's anything unique about human intelligence.

I loved college.

MICROMAN'S WEALTH ACCUMULATION SINCE MICROSOFT WENT PUBLIC ON MARCH 13, 1986	
UNIT OF TIME	DOLLARS MADE
Seconds	$146.05
Minutes	$8,763.01
Hours	$525,780.74
Days	$12.62 Million
Weeks	$88.33 Million
Months	$378.56 Million
Years	$4.61 Billion

source: Marcus, Evan. The Bill Gates Net Worth Page.

MICROSOFT

I'm sure that one of the reasons I was so determined to help develop the personal computer is that I wanted one for myself.

There was no doubt in my mind we could write a BASIC. It was kind of funny because we were sort of acting like we had it already.

NUMBERS OF MICROSOFT EMPLOYEES

1975: 4
1978: about 16
1984: about 475
1994: about 15,000
1996: more than 20,000

You and Paul decided to leave computer hardware in the hands of companies who had already established themselves. But if you were right, and the move to microcomputers was inevitable, those new, small, cheap computers would need software to make them run properly. Something easy, like BASIC (Beginner's All-purpose Symbolic Instruction Code), a simple programming language that enables programmers to write more complex programs for a system. So you wrote letters to computer companies, offering to write a version of BASIC for the new, powerful Intel chip. There were no takers.

Your big break: the release, in 1975, of the MITS (Micro Instrumentation Telemetry Systems) Altair. You and Paul read about the new computer, which was powered by the new Intel chip, in *Popular Electronics*. Just as you had predicted, though, the computer was not much good to anyone because it had no software to make it work.

Your first strike: the development of BASIC that allowed the MITS Altair to operate. You and Paul contacted the makers of the Altair and told them that you had a version of BASIC already written. They

THE CUSTOMER IS ALWAYS RIGHT

In 1984, after the release of Microsoft Multiplan for the Apple Macintosh, the Multiplan team discovered a major bug. You authorized the shipping of free, corrected programs to every customer. Price tag: a quarter of a million dollars.

Microbasics **Microjobs** Microvisits Microvehicles Microhome
Microplay Microriches Micropolitics Microgiving Microfolk
Microreligion Microworries Microdreams Microimage Microman

25

wanted it. Which meant you had to get to work
developing the program that you had promised,
since despite all the thought you had put into the
program, you had not written it yet.

As a result, you and Paul became the world's first
software company programming for microcomputers.

In the beginning, Microsoft was called Micro-Soft
(you decided against Allen & Gates Inc.). It was
formed on April 4, 1975. Paul Allen had proved con-
vincing enough to get you – nineteen years old and
with dreams of fame and fortune – out of Harvard
and into the infancy of the computer technology
business. The two of you took off for Albuquerque,
New Mexico to set up shop. That first Microsoft office
contained four people: you, Paul, and two high school
friends, Marc McDonald and Ric Weiland, the latter a
member of your earlier company, the Lakeside Programmers Group.

Albuquerque was the place to be. As the home of
MITS it enabled you to be in direct contact with the
makers of the first microcomputer, and you saw this as
the beginning of a new age, an era when computers
would become faster, more powerful, and cheaper, all
at the same time. This was the dawning of a technological revolution. You were in on it from the beginning.

What else about Albuquerque appealed to you?
The lack of distraction? The cheap cost of living? Was
it as simple as your loving to drive your car at breakneck speeds? Those desert flats were perfect for racing, and you took full advantage. One of your cars
was dubbed "Dune Buggy" because you spun it out in
a sand drift during a late night trek.

Eighty percent of the improvements in products like Windows result from customer feedback.

Yet, there is no toll-free phone number for cus-tomers to call. If anyone is in trouble, has a problem they can't fix, they pay to call you for help with your software.

Now THAT's customer service.

Pretty quickly we decided that we ought to get out [to Albu-querque] and really help these guys get their act together.

You may not have had much time for such frivolity, though. When you weren't furiously writing code you were taking care of the business: tracking taxes, doing accounting and payroll, and selling software. Before long, MITS wasn't the only company making microcomputers. By 1977, the TRS-80, the Commodore PET, and the Apple II were hitting the market. Although these machines were first released to consumers with in-house software, within a year they had all licensed your BASIC. This was your first taste of establishing a standard.

In 1979, the company had grown too big for New Mexico and you and Paul moved Microsoft home to Seattle: the place of your birth, the home of your family. Maybe you thought that by living in a rainy climate you wouldn't feel so bad about asking your employees to spend all their time inside. Maybe it was so you could take advantage of contacts that your parents could introduce you to.

Your first major alliance: with IBM in 1980. IBM was looking for an operating system for their new personal computers. Other software companies were considered, but your MS-DOS was chosen. But did you do it alone? John Opel, who was at the time IBM chairman, knew your mother. They had worked together on the national board of the United Way.

What IBM may not have known was that MS-DOS wasn't a Microsoft program to begin with. You had seen Q-DOS, produced by Seattle Computer Products, which you knew was a hot ticket. You licensed the program, then bought it outright. Q-DOS became MS-DOS.

IBM was very good to Microsoft, and you and your

We wanted to be part of that excitement. (on your move to Albuquerque)

Most of our early customers were out of business fairly early on.

If things hadn't worked out, I could always go back to school. I was officially on leave. (on the early days of Microsoft)

A company should have short-term goals, of course. But long-term goals and strategies are essential to long-term success.

Microbasics **Microjobs** Microvisits Microvehicles Microhome
Microplay Microfiches Micropolitics Microgiving Microfolk
Microreligion Microworries Microdreams Microimage Microman

27

colleagues did everything you could to cater to the whims of the over-sized conglomerate, agreeing to help them develop a next-level operating system called OS/2. But their bureaucracy – and their seeming lack of understanding of the new computer age – wore you and the Microsoft programmers down. You asked them to leave the software development to you. They refused, so you did what you could, and had other Microsoft staff working on Windows. You were going to make sure you were in on the next generation. In May, 1990, Microsoft was ready to put Windows 3.0 on the market and you asked IBM to use it instead of OS/2. Again they refused, and a couple of years later, Microsoft broke ties with Big Blue. It was either that or get caught in a nowhere development. And you had places to go, things to do. OS/2 wasn't one of them.

We are a very predictable company. *(on Microsoft)*

Our business relationship with IBM was vital to us.

Microsoft incorporated on June 25, 1981 and went public on March 13, 1986, the same day you and the gang moved into the corporate campus that now epitomizes Microsoft. You become a millionaire overnight and that day marks the beginning of your roller coaster ride in the carnival of fame and fortune.

Death can come swiftly to a market leader.

You believed, way back in the late seventies, that the most complex computer tasks could be performed by smaller, personal computers instead of huge mainframe systems. Your predictions were coming true, and Microsoft was going to capitalize on this movement by providing the software that would enable this to happen.

We were doubling every two years.... The profits went up the same way. *(on the early growth of Microsoft)*

And while you maintained that Microsoft was not going to be getting into the business of develop-

"[You were] very humble and would speak softer [with IBM]. There was a definite difference in the tone of [your] voice. ... You'd go in the meeting and it was just a fascinating contrast to see [you] at IBM versus [you] at any of the other companies." [You] would even wear a suit and tie.
— Edstrom & Eller

[You] knew better than anyone else just how much IBM's reflected glory meant to Microsoft. By endorsing DOS in 1981, IBM had instantaneously turned Microsoft into a major player.
— Edstrom & Eller

Microsoft wears the personality of its leader like a wet suit.
— James Gleick

ing hardware or providing Internet access, you were leading the company into the realm of "content": providing the information that people would be accessing.

It was a logical step. Just as software and applications are the "content" for computers and their hardware, "content" for the Internet and the information highway is made up of words, pictures, sounds, and how those things are displayed on screens.

AN ABBREVIATED HISTORY OF MICROSOFT

"When Ronald Reagan became President, [your] new company was an unincorporated partnership with accounts kept in handwritten ledgers. Apple was a big new personal-computer company; IBM, the mainframe giant, was cobbling together its first personal computer out of parts from outside suppliers. By 1990, just a decade later, Microsoft had become the world's richest software company, though it had no leading product in any important category but operating systems. Today nearly half of the world's total PC software revenue goes directly to Microsoft. ... The vast majority of the world's personal computers – estimates range from 80 percent to more than 90 percent – run on Microsoft software from the instant they are turned on."

source: Gleick, James.

Microbasics **Microjobs** Microvisits Microvehicles Microhome
Microplay Microriches Micropolitics Microgiving Microfolk
Microreligion Microworries Microdreams Microimage Microman

29

APPLE

In 1984 Microsoft and Apple were buddies. You took the back seat to Steve Jobs, who was the computer industry's golden boy at the time (before being forced out, and then brought back again). Knowing that Apple's Macintosh computer was light-years ahead of any other personal computer, you wanted to make sure that you were providing the software for each and every Mac in the market.

One of the elements of the Macintosh that was so appealing was its on-screen display. It was user-friendly, representing computer functions with picures. Those in the industry called it a "graphical user interface." People didn't have to understand obscure computer programming languages to be able to use Apple computers. You knew this was important and, trying to help Apple maintain its control of the industry, you offered to help them out. In 1985, you wrote a memo to Apple suggesting that they license their operating system. What you were suggesting was that by giving permission to a few companies for them to make Macintosh-compatible computers, not only would Apple receive money for royalties, but the Macintosh and Macintosh-like machines would flood the market, and become the standard.

While the Apple executives weren't sure how they could make this work, you had been licensing software for a few years, and understood how it could benefit Apple. So you offered to help them. At a Las Vegas Comdex trade show, you told author Jim Carlton that you were willing to "facilitate it by being a middleman." You went so far as to make phone calls to senior executives you knew at AT&T and Hewlett-Packard, asking them if they would be interested in licensing the Apple operating system. They were.

Your rationale for offering to help Apple was simple. "Understand, you make a lot more money selling applications than you do operating systems," you explained to Carlton. So, you were offering to help Apple take over the market, because then you could make money providing software for those

Until 1983, the computer industry ... had no idea ... when it came to packaging and pitching products for consumers. [You], in the early 1980s, [were] the epitome of this clueless arrogance.
– Edstrom & Eller

People didn't believe in graphical interface. Apple bet their company on it.... We thought they were right. And we really bet our success on it as well.

Researchers at Xerox's now-famous Palo-Alto Research Center ... showed that it was easier to instruct a computer if you could point at things on the screen and see pictures.

Business isn't that complicated. ... Say you added two years to my life and let me go to business school. I don't think I would have done a better job at Microsoft.

computers. Who made the computers wasn't important to you, because your software would run on the Macintosh or the Macintosh-clones. It didn't matter.

But while Apple was developing the Mac, you and Microsoft were also working on a new operating system. Eventually called Windows, it also used pictures to represent functions. When the big-wigs at Apple caught wind of this they threatened legal action, but because you were making software for their computers, you were able to strike a deal. You licensed the Macintosh interface; you secured permission to make Windows "look and feel" like a Macintosh.

While you've always maintained that both you and Apple took the idea of the graphical user interface from earlier Xerox technology, that license made it easy, and legal, for you to take Windows into the future. Microsoft became more than just a software company. It set the industry standard for operating systems. Virtually all computers would run Windows, and nearly all software would have to be written to run on Windows. All of a sudden you had it all.

It was a winning formula. The more programs were written for Windows, the more copies of Windows you could sell. And the more copies of Windows you could sell, the more programs would have to be written to run on Windows. Instead of just making money by selling programs, you'd make money selling the operating systems, too. The money-making spiral began. It was 1989.

Make no mistake: [You are] no softy as a businessman.
— Forbes, *April, 1991*

Microbasics **Microjobs** Microvisits Microvehicles Microhome
Microplay Microriches Micropolitics Microgiving Microfolk
Microreligion Microworries Microdreams Microimage Microman

31

APPLE UPDATE

In August 1997, you shocked the industry by announcing Microsoft's investment in Apple to the tune of $150 million. Once people adjusted to their surprise, the deal made sense. Not only were you perceived as a "savior" for helping out your long-time ally, but you ensured that Microsoft would continue being the number one supplier of software for Apple computers.

Apple and Microsoft, together again. You've settled the old disputes, and everyone marches on with *big* smiles.

Working for [you] had been like white-water rafting, not ocean cruising. There were so many other near misses and episodes of dumb luck that the public and Microsoft investors never knew about.
– *Edstrom & Eller*

According to *Fortune*, with 1997 revenues of over $11 billion, Microsoft placed #2 on the list of America's Most Admired Companies, and #8 on the list of Best Companies to Work For in America. The Microsoft stock-option plan has created more than 100 millionaires among Microsoft employees.

[You] may be the hardest-working man in big business.
– Fortune, *May 26, 1997*

Corporate reorganizations may be prompted by failures now and then, but more often they are essential elements of success.

MICROSOFT EXTRAS

Content is where I expect much of the real money will be made on the Internet.

If you were Bill Gates you would want your company to diversify. So you guided Microsoft beyond software and into other realms of content. Entertainment is the money-maker of the past, present, and future, and, especially because it is "software," you want Microsoft to be involved in the production and distribution of it all. And because the Internet is such an important vehicle for entertainment, you've got Microsoft in deep.

Slate (www.slate.com)

Slate is the on-line magazine associated with Microsoft. Articles, commentary, graphics: all are available. For a price. Although a few headlines and teasers are available for free, to get the real deal a person has to subscribe. Just like with a real magazine. Nothin' for free.

We're in this for the long haul. (on the failure of Slate *to generate profits)*

Slate should not be confused with other on-line publications such as *Suck* or *Feed*. *Slate* boasts – actually lists in their advertisements – columns, stories, poems, and commentary by such notable figures as writers Mavis Gallant and Douglas Coupland, critic Susan Faludi, film-guy Roger Ebert (the "robust" thumb), humorist David Sedaris, and dead poets Wallace Stevens and William Butler Yeats. According to George Stephanopoulos, political wonderboy, everyone at the White House reads *Slate*.

Microbasics **Microjobs** Microvisits Microvehicles Microhome
Microplay Microriches Micropolitics Microgiving Microfolk
Microreligion Microworries Microdreams Microimage Microman

33

MSNBC (www.msnbc.com)

With culture, entertainment, opinion and the like covered by *Slate*, you made sure to get the news angle on things by getting Microsoft into a deal with NBC, the television network. Hard facts on world events. They even had a full series of reports on you and the government: "Justice vs. Microsoft."

WebTV (*www.webtv.com*)

They call themselves "the pioneer and leader of the Internet television market." While they've only been around for a couple of years – and were officially acquired by Microsoft on August 1, 1997 – WebTV has collected a few subscribers for their service, which turns a television into a computer monitor, allowing you to use your favorite 40-inch television to surf the Internet or watch specialty programming provided over the Internet.

DreamWorks Interactive

On March 22, 1995 a big alliance in the entertainment industry was announced. Steven Spielberg, David Geffen, and Jeffrey Katzenberg, who together make up DreamWorks SKG, a powerful company involved in the production of motion pictures, television, and music, teamed up with you in deciding that multimedia – entertainment software – was a good place for you all to be. DreamWorks Interactive was formed, bringing together the skills of movie indus-

MSNBC has become so cool, so "today," that it is even showing up in Hollywood. Tea Leoni's character in the 1998 film *Deep Impact* is an anchor for MSNBC. She keeps America up-to-date on Earth's collision course with a massive asteriod.

After compiling their statistics from the fall of 1997, the Nielsen television ratings company announced that fewer people watched television because they were on-line. In a similar study, Coopers & Lybrand reported that fifty-eight percent of Internet users admitted that they sacrifice television viewing time to go online.

Steven Spielberg has confirmed that the fourth Indiana Jones movie will begin shooting in the summer of 2000 with Harrison Ford and Sean Connery. "The *Indiana Jones 4* hat is halfway on my head," Spielberg told the *Chicago Tribune*. "I have the plot worked out."

In its January 1994 cover story, the *American Bar Association Journal* states: "Presently, more studies exist that appear to link EMF exposure [from appliances like cellular phones] to an increased risk of cancer than existed linking asbestos exposure to an increased rate of cancer at a similar embryonic stage of asbestos litigation."

try animators and designers with the programming skills and market domination of Microsoft.

If you were Bill Gates your chances of getting to star in a Spielberg feature film increased dramatically. The question everyone wants to know the answer to is: "Can you act?"

MOONLIGHTING

Time, so valuable to you, must never be wasted. rather than wiling away the hours in front of the television, you keep yourself more than occcupied with a number of second jobs. You are one busy fellow.

Comcast (*www.comcast.com*)

Specialty programming delivered to consumers over the Internet just might come from another company you partially own, Comcast, which is a "diversified global leader in entertainment services and telecommunications." Comcast runs cable television and telephone companies and provides cellular phone service and satellite TV programming. They also own QVC, a home-shopping network that gives people a chance to buy stuff over their television or computer, and with Disney own E! Entertainment Television, a cable network.

Teledesic (*www.teledesic.com*)

Microsoft might not be getting into the Internet server business, but you are. Why not make some

Microbasics **Microjobs** Microvisits Microvehicles Microhome
Microplay Microriches Micropolitics Microgiving Microfolk
Microreligion Microworries Microdreams Microimage Microman

35

money off what Microsoft wants to do and have some say in how the communication industry develops? You became an investor in Teledesic, which intends to establish, around the world, a broadband, two-way telecommunications service.

It's a radical idea, expensive and some might say a little too science fiction for its own good. But that isn't stopping you. By the year 2002, Teledesic intends to launch 288 satellites into orbit around the earth. The idea is to create a net of satellites – kind of like Reagan's Star Wars – but this net would provide wireless connection for communications and, especially, the Internet, from anywhere in the world. It's being hailed as an "Internet-in-the-Sky." Teledesic wants to move information hundreds of times faster than contemporary modems. You and Teledesic launched your first test satellite on February 25, 1998.

Corbis (*www.corbis.com*)

You founded Corbis in 1989, although it was originally called Continuum. The company is entirely unaffiliated with Microsoft. It's yours. You own it. Its three hundred employees work for you and you alone.

The idea was to "build a premiere collection of digitized art and photography." It was an opportunity to preserve and catalogue visual images, many of which are historically and culturally important. Corbis now has over 1.3 million images in its collection.

Corbis purchases the rights to pictures – photographs, paintings, drawings, etchings – then digitizes them using computer scanners. By converting the

NASA, the United States' National Aeronautics and Space Administration, has an annual budget of $13.08 billion. You alone could finance the U.S. space effort for over four years.

source: Marcus, Evan. The Bill Gates Net Worth Page.

Voyager 1, launched in September, 1977, is currently 9.39 billion kilometers (5.83 billion miles) from Earth. Voyager 2, launched in August 1977, is currently 7.21 billion kilometers (4.48 billion miles) away. They are expected to be in operating condition until the year 2015.

images to digital form you enable easy cataloguing and searching of images. If someone wants to find a picture of the stone statues on Easter Island, they simply visit the Corbis site and type "Easter Island" into the search box. Behold! Pictures of Easter Island available, for a price, of course. And there are pictures of Rasputin, too.

Corbis is Latin for "woven basket."

There are two parts to Corbis: the side that licenses images, and the side that produces, or publishes, material. The licensing side has secured the rights to images from prestigious galleries and artists such as the Bettmann Archive, Ansel Adams, even the paintings of the Hermitage in St. Petersburg. And because you purchased, for $30.8 million, Leonardo da Vinci's *Codex Leicester* – a collection of writings and drawings created in the 16th century – Corbis has access to the images from that book as well.

Killer applications help technological advances change from curiosities into moneymaking essentials.

The publication arm of Corbis is earning the money that the licensing side spends. They do this by producing interactive CD-ROMs – such as *Leonardo da Vinci* – Internet projects, and as a stock photo agency, selling image rights to designers, art directors, and other print and new media publishers.

The only field I'll ever make a world-class contribution in, if any, is software.

Despite what some people think, your Corbis is not the only company in the world buying up image rights. You have competitors, the biggest of which is Getty Images in London.

Darwin Molecular (*www.darwin.com*)

You are a futurist in every sense. Not only are you directing the future of computers and software, but

Microbasics **Microjobs** Microvisits Microvehicles Microhome
Microplay Microriches Micropolitics Microgiving Microfolk
Microreligion Microworries Microdreams Microimage Microman

37

you are also fascinated with genetics. You are a share-
holder in Darwin Molecular, a biotechnology company that is involved with human gene mapping.

This all makes perfect sense. People are made up
of genes just as computers are made up of circuits.
You and your teams already know all about computers, and if our brains operate sort of like computers,
as some scientists suggest, who wouldn't want to
figure out the circuitry of the human body?

ICOS Corporation (*www.icos.com*)

Continuing with the medical research themes that
seem to interest you, you sit on the board of directors
of ICOS, a company dedicated to researching, developing, and "commercializing" pharmaceuticals for
treating "inflammatory diseases and other serious
medical conditions."

I think I'd be working
in biotechnology.
*(on what you'd be
doing if not working
in computers)*

After the interna-
tional community
learned about
"Dolly," the cloned
sheep, research
partner PPL Thera-
peutic's share
price rose by fifty
percent, President
Clinton asked the
bioethics commis-
sion to report on
the ethical impli-
cations of her exis-
tence, and
researchers
received requests
to resurrect rela-
tives and pets.

MICROMAN: INVENTOR

In 1996, people had fun mocking you for your patented
(U.S. Patent 5,552,982) "method and system for processing fields in a document processor." Essentially it is a
computer program that enables users to merge
addresses from a database with a letter, allowing
them to have form letters with personalized greetings.
The funny thing is that while word processors in the
early eighties had this feature, nobody secured a
patent on it until you did. Just like Apple and their
graphical operating system. Someone missed a step
and you capitalized on it.

All the neurons in the
brain that make up
perceptions and emo-
tions operate in a
binary fashion.

Columnist

On January 3, 1995 your first column for the *New York Times* was published. You talked about how communication has changed in the past twenty years: now we have electronic mail. You said: "Think of this new column as my e-mail to you."

Every month since then your column has appeared – also showing up in electronic form on the Microsoft website (www.microsoft.com/BillGates) and the *New York Times* site (nytsyn.com/live/Gates). You write a special column on December 31. Sort of a look back, a look ahead kind of thing.

Author

You are also an author, although you had help writing your book that looks at the future of computers and society (*The Road Ahead* was written with Microsoft's Nathan Myhrvold and Peter Rinearson). The book cover, with a photo by Annie Leibowitz, shows you standing in the middle of an endless highway – a folksy metaphor for the information highway – that stretches out behind you. Hands in your pockets, you look back at the reader, casually suggesting that you are the one to guide them down that road. Just be sure to watch for the vehicles that will be zipping up and down that road. The coyote is bound to catch the roadrunner some day.

Maybe you are Moses. Maybe you are the Pied Piper. Maybe you are simply the lemming in front, heading directly for the edge.

During the *Murphy Brown* series finale, Candice Bergen's Murphy Brown character gets a chance to interview God. As she is about to enter God's office, his public relations staff advise her not to ask any questions about Bill Gates. "God sold Microsoft much too early," they explain.

Microbasics **Microjobs** Microvisits Microvehicles Microhome
Microplay Microriches Micropolitics Microgiving Microfolk
Microreligion Microworries Microdreams Microimage Microman

39

The book itself is a trip into the future through your eyes, a story which, as you promised a *Playboy* interviewer, is "about the future instead of the past." What will life be like for us next year? In ten years? You admit freely that your powers of prophesy are hardly comparable to those of Nostradamus, but the bestseller status of the book suggests that readers around the world are curious to know what you think, what you have to say.

Sometimes I rock back and forth or pace when I'm thinking, because it helps me focus on a single idea and exclude distractions.

Of course a CD-ROM accompanies the book. It contains the complete text from the book with links to sound and video clips, an interview with you, and even a browser so readers can go right from your book to the Internet. You say you're just trying to make life easier for the reader by including the browser. Why shouldn't they get more bang for their buck? Competitors claim that it is another sneaky strategy to get your free software into consumer hands so they won't pay for a competing browser.

Keynote Speaker

Not only do you write, you talk. Lots. But you have moved from talking with friends over beer and pizza to talking with employees to talking to thousands of people at conferences and seminars. On your trip to India and South America in 1997, you presented fourteen formal speeches.

[Your] speeches didn't really dazzle anyone; they were informative and to the point but showed little verve or showmanship.
– Fortune, *May 26, 1997*

You've spoken at Comdex, at the Newspaper Association of America's Publisher Convention, at the World Economic Forum, and at Consumer Electronics. You've spoken to industry leaders, politicians,

For my first major talk [in 1981], "speaker support" consisted of my dad, who operated the slide projector.

journalists, and community college students. You've spoken in New York, Atlanta, New Orleans, Chicago, Orlando, Las Vegas, Washington, Toronto, Sydney, Beijing, Tokyo, Paris, and Cambridge.

You haven't always been this popular. Based on the speeches listed on your webpage (www. microsoft.com/BillGates) you only delivered one speech in 1994, two in 1995, and thirteen in 1996. In 1997, you spoke thirty-one times. By May of 1998, you had already delivered twenty speeches, most of those to the major computer and technology industry convention and trade shows. You are in demand.

Microvisits

Around the World in Economy Class

If you were Bill Gates you've always been on the road and it seems that you are always on the road for work. Bussing to Pullman, Washington to visit Paul while he was at university, flying to Boston then over to Cambridge after you enrolled at Harvard, driving to Albuquerque, New Mexico to set-up your first Microsoft office, driving back home to Seattle to build the first Microsoft "campus."

Soon after you and Paul had formed Microsoft and were developing BASIC for the Altair, you initiated a grand road trip around the country to start computer clubs and popularize the new technology. Your road trip led to the formation of thirty computer clubs around America, most in California.

It takes a long time for people to change the pattern of how they buy things.

You don't like to waste money on travel. When flying in North America you sit in the commercial section with the rest of the regulars. Flying overseas, however, you need the extra space of business class

to accommodate your books and your laptop computer. No need to waste time just sitting there.

In January 1997, you were in Zurich. Then, a few months later, you travelled to India and South Africa. That meant you were high in the sky for however long it took to travel 25,000 miles. As the crow flies. The trip was successful, you say, because you had something to do every minute. No wasted time.

You don't take time to see the sights. What you glimpse from a car window as you speed past a landmark is sufficient. But you are always asking questions, accumulating information to add to what you've read on the flight over, getting to know the new place you're in.

In March 1998, you were off to Australia and Southeast Asia. In Australia and Singapore you paid homage to countries that are quickly becoming com-

> The global marketplace is replacing the U.S. marketplace as the one that really matters.

DON'T WASTE YOUR TIME!

Consider that you have made your money in the twenty-three years since Microsoft was founded in 1975. If we presume that you have worked fourteen hours a day on every business day of the year since then, that means you've been making money at a staggering half-million dollars per hour, around $150 per second.

Which means that if, on your way into the office, should you see or drop a $500 bill on the ground, it's just not worth your time to bend over and pick it up. You would make more just heading off to work.

source: Templeton, Brad. Bill Gates Wealth Index.

˙ Microbasics Microjobs **Microvisits** Microvehicles Microhome
Microplay Microriches Micropolitics Microgiving Microfolk
Microreligion Microworries Microdreams Microimage Microman

43

pletely hard-wired (with fiber-optics) communities. In Malaysia and the Philippines, you were likely checking to see how hard it was going to be to continue growing as the Asian economy collapsed.

Sometimes you travel for fun. A vacation. In November 1995, you and friends travelled to China. You say you didn't even take your laptop computer with you but no one believes it. You rode bikes and visited Tiananmen Square, the Great Wall, the terra-cotta warriors at Xi'an. You were a tourist.

As you were guided around the Forbidden City, absorbing the history of that ancient place, you were shown massive scrolls that you could look at but not touch. Imagining how unbearable life would have been without computers, you watched as the scrolls were unrolled by trained staff and held up for you to see. Trying to read the text must have been like an average computer user trying to understand the error messages that flash on their screens when their computer crashes. You turned to your friends, as the scrolls were being carefully rolled up, and muttered, "There's a two dollar fine if you return a scroll not rewound."

But despite all the flying and travelling you do,

MICROMAN AS A COUNTRY		
RANK	COUNTRY	1995 GDP
1	U.S.	$5.45 Trillion
2	Japan	$3.01 Trillion
3	Germany	$1.5 Trillion
36	Malaysia	$62.4 Billion
37	Israel	$58.84 Billion
38	Venezuela	$57.37 Billion
	Microman	$56.85 Billion
39	Greece	$53.23 Billion
40	Ukraine	$51.76 Billion
41	Portugal	$51.4 Billion

source: Marcus, Evan. The Bill Gates Net Worth Page.

I never realized that there are 14 distinct written and spoken languages in India. Now that I understand that, we're going to invest a whole lot more in localizing our products. A billion people is a lot of people.

A vacation, by definition, is a period in which you get immersed in something that's broader and different than what you do normally.

there is no Gates Lear, no Microsoft Gulfstream. You say it's because you don't want to get used to it.

You're still trying to live like a regular, "normal" person. How long can it last?

I wish I were a kid again. (on what technology offers children)

Microsoft staff photo, 1978.

Microvehicles

Faster Car, Go! Go!

If you were Bill Gates you would love driving. Fast.

You have a reputation for getting lots of speeding tickets, pinning the needle above 170 miles per hour. When you were living in Albuquerque you used to race your cars in the desert. When you were driving from Albuquerque to Seattle (why fly when you can drive?) you got three speeding tickets, two from the same cop.

I never get bored.

You've owned Porsches (a 911, a 930 Turbo, a 959, a Carrera Cabriolet 964), a Mercedes, a Jaguar xj6, and a Ferrari 348. Now you drive a Lexus. Not as much of a sports car as the others, but you're a family man, now.

Despite your enormous wealth, you shun a chauffeur-driven limosine and instead drive yourself. When you get home you park in the thirty-car garage in your new house (more on the house later). You still have the red Mustang convertible that you drove after getting your license. It belonged to your parents.

I get fewer speeding tickets than I used to.

You still spend a long weekend every spring with a friend in North Carolina where you ride dune buggies. You feel the need for speed.

PICKING UP THEM DOLLAR BILLS

Imagine an endless line of one dollar bills laid end to end. If someone began traveling along this line picking up dollar bills since the day Microsoft went public, and that person wanted to accumulate wealth at the same rate you have since that date, they would need to travel along that line picking up dollar bills at 50.95 mph or 82 kph.

source: Marcus, Evan. The Bill Gates Net Worth Page.

COMPARATIVE WEALTH

Another way to examine your wealth is to compare it to an average American of reasonable but modest wealth. Perhaps they have a net worth of $100,000. Your worth is 400,000 times larger. Which means that if something costs one hundred thousand dollars to them, to you it's as though it costs twenty-five cents. A new Lambourghini Diablo costs $250,000. In Bill Dollars that's only sixty-three cents. A topline, fully-loaded laptop costs a penny. A nice home in a rich town like Palo Alto, California? Two dollars. That nice mansion in Seattle? A more reasonable $125 to you.

Someone else might spend a hundred dollars on tickets, food, and parking to take their family to see an NHL hockey game. You, on the other hand, could buy the team for one hundred Bill-bills.

source: Templeton, Brad. Bill Gates Wealth Index.

IT'S A MATTER OF PROPORTION

Assuming an average American's net worth of $70,000

TRANSACTION	PROPORTIONAL CHANGE TO AVERAGE AMERICAN'S NET WORTH	PROPORTIONAL CHANGE TO YOUR NET WORTH
Find a penny on the sidewalk	+1¢	+$8,121.58
Dig 30¢ from the cushions of the couch	+30¢	+$243,647.65
See a current movie with a date	-$16	-$12.99 Million
Have a moderate dinner for two	-$40	-$32.49 Million
Make a lease payment on a car	-$239	-$194.11 Million
Pay the mortgage	-$1500	-$1.22 Billion
Buy a house	-$175,000	-$142.13 Billion
Buy an average car	-$12,000	-$9.75 Billion
Hit the lottery for $10 Million	+$10,000,000	+$8.12 Trillion

source: Marcus, Evan. The Bill Gates Net Worth Page.

Microhome

The Fortress

There is really only one house for you. It sits on the shore of Lake Washington in Medina, an upper-class suburb of Seattle, built on a five-acre section of land.

This house was important when you first conceived it in the late 1980s. You had been living the true campus life, spending more time at the office than at home, staying out all hours. You didn't really have a base of operations. But you were approaching forty and it didn't look like the money was going to go away. The house was something you could do with all that money. You wouldn't buy a plane, but you would build a house. You decided to build a house that had every feature you could ever want.

It was a good thing you had made arrangements for more permanent accommodations. Your new family was going to have to live somewhere, and they might as well live in opulence.

Originally planned for completion in 1994, con-

I'm building a house. It has serious functions, but entertainment is most of it.

struction was delayed by changes to plans. Many of the changes came about after you married Melinda French and she asserted her right to have a say in things – by adding bedrooms for children, for example. The original $10 million price tag has ballooned beyond comprehension – in true Microman fashion – to over $50 million.

$50 million for a house! Well, they say money is only as good as what you spend it on.

Sexually explicit content is as old as information itself.
(on the Internet)

THE COST OF
HIGH LIVING

LAND PURCHASE
$9,122,200

BUILDING COSTS
$53,392,200

PROPERTY TAXES
(1997) $620,183

SELLING FEATURES

4 bedrooms

10 full bathrooms

nanny's quarters

6 kitchens

6 fireplaces

heated floors

3 garages, the biggest of which is built into the hillside and can hold thirty cars

17- × 60-foot pool with underwater speakers

caretaker's residence and guest cottage

1,900-square foot office and reception area

1,000-square foot formal dining room

20-seat movie theatre with popcorn maker

2,100-square foot library (being stocked by a rare-book dealer)

lakeside pavillion

2,500-square foot excercise room with sauna, steam room, men's & women's lockers

trampoline room with 20-foot ceiling

multi-sport court and putting green

You have built your fortune on computers and technology so it makes sense that they feature prominently. The house has a brain: a 100-computer-network-centre within the building, connected by miles of cable, that controls most of its features. Each room has wall screens – to display digitized still images (art, photographs, video captures – many from Corbis) and moving pictures (television, movies, videos) – and speakers, all connected to the central brain.

We've been a big proponent of relaxed immigration rules.

Like any other person with money to burn, you have been collecting art. da Vinci's *Codex Leicester* was only the beginning. You went on, in 1998, to buy the last Winslow Homer painting still in private hands. *Lost on the Grand Banks* – a "dramatic" oil painting by the acclaimed American artist who died in 1883 – only cost you thirty million dollars. The difference between you and others is that you seem to prefer to have the art available to you in electronic form so it can be displayed on a wall screen. You bring new meaning to the term *nouveau riche*.

The most innovative and space-age feature is the "smart" pins, which will be worn by you and your guests to the house. (Do they *have* to?) Just like communicator pins in *Star Trek: The Next Generation*, the "smart" pins will communicate – by wireless – with the central computer and will be personalized. So as you move from one area of the house to another, the computer tracks you from room to room, raising light and temperature to your preferred levels. With telephones in every room, and because the computer system knows where you are, only the phone in the

That [not eating meat] was only a three-year period when I was proving to myself I could do it.

room you are in will ring. And having indicated your favorite music, images, and movies to the central computer, as you move from room to room the brain will make you comfortable by fulfilling your entertainment desires. Elsewhere in the house, where other people with other favorites are milling about, different music and pictures will be available.

The big question: what happens when people with conflicting tastes enter the same room? You have indicated that the central computer will be programmed to respond to a hierarchy. So you, being the king of the castle, get to see your favourite pictures and hear your favourite songs. A great strategy to deal with an annoying reporter asking stupid questions, but maybe not so gracious for your guests, who may prefer Stereolab over the Stones.

The computer brain not only centralizes the features of the house, and makes them accessible anywhere within the house, but it learns, too. So the more times a guest visits your house, the better the brain gets to know him and his tastes in art and music. As long as they don't change their minds very often.

The house is equipped with a 2,300-square foot reception hall for entertaining. It can seat 150 people for dinner, or 200 people for a standing-room party. On one wall are twenty-four forty-inch rear projection television monitors in a grid, creating a twenty-two-foot video display. Perfect for showing the latest Microsoft product demos.

But you are in the Pacific Northwest – an earthquake zone, on the edge of the Pacific Rim, along the Ring of Fire. To protect your new home massive

If you have everything centralized, it's a lot easier to manage things.

I went to [your] house, and [your] vcr is still flashing 12:00.
– Jay Leno, at the Windows 95 launch

Microbasics Microjobs Microvisits Microvehicles **Microhome**
Microplay Microriches Micropolitics Microgiving Microfolk
Microreligion Microworries Microdreams Microimage Microman

53

retaining walls provide a secure base for the structures. You'll be safe when the "Big One" hits.

Although technology is integral to your house, you have made a concerted effort to maintain a natural look and feel. After all, you grew up in the Pacific Northwest. You have an appreciation for trees and green grass and water. The beams of the house were constructed from 500-year-old Douglas fir timbers salvaged from an old lumber mill that was being torn down. More than half a million feet of wood was used in the house's construction.

And at your lakefront, your shoreline, is a bonafide wetlands, where a small estuary flows groundwater into Lake Washington, a natural home for fish, ducks, even otters. It will be stocked with salmon and sea-run cutthroat trout.

Were these decisions – recycling wood, creating a habitat for wildlife – just for show? To maintain a positive image? Had you really thought about minimizing your impact on the environment or were you just doing what someone else suggested? There is no tangible payback for you. Fish don't use computers. How does your conscience respond to this?

One story on the Internet tells that the first night you stayed in your new house, the central computer brain suffered from a few crossed neurons, and you couldn't get the lights to turn off. That didn't faze you, though. There are simply too many things to do at your new house. Why waste the time trying to sleep with the lights on?

If my discipline ever broke down it would confuse me.... So I try to prevent that.

DEEP PILE CARPETING

With your cache of dollar bills, you could place them flat on the found so they didn't overlap. You would cover an area of 142,246 acres, or 222 miles. You could cover with dollar bills the surface area of:

- Manhattan, NY 10 times
- Vatican City 1,308 times

source: Marcus, Evan. The Bill Gates Net Worth Page.

Microman and
Melinda as
spectators, 1993.

Microplay

The Leisure Suit Life

You've always loved computers and twenty years ago you turned your biggest hobby into a career. That must have left you searching for something to do when you weren't working.

As technology increases our efficiency, we will have extra time to engage in leisure activities with one another.

You played the board game Risk as a kid. In hindsight the game's goal of world domination seems like the perfect practice field. Take no prisoners, as they say. But you've aged, matured, changed. Now you work on puzzles, and play golf and bridge. And you do all of these things with the same energy and will to succeed that you do everything. You focus on achieving goals: making Microsoft software an industry standard and lowering your handicap.

[You love] games that involve problem solving.

– Warren Buffett

You really enjoy the intellectual challenges that puzzles provide. And you become all-consumed by such challenges: whether solving complex mathematical matrices on your own or playing nine-hour games of bridge with friends.

BUYING POWER

ITEM	COST	NUMBER YOU CAN AFFORD
Cream Pies	$7.95	7.15 Billion
Copy of Windows 98	$89.95	632 Million
Viagra Tablets	$10	5,685,111,907 *(at one per day this will last you over 15.5 Million years)*
Titanic: the movie	$200 Million	284
Boeing 747-400	$156 Million	364
Michael Jordan's Bulls Salary	$30 Million	1,895
1998 Bentley Continental	$343,900	165,312
1997 Geo Metro	$8605	6.61 Million
Four years tuition, room, and board at Harvard	$115,584	491,860

source: *Marcus, Evan. The Bill Gates Net Worth Page.*

[You] got into golf in the same addictive way [you] get into anything else. It gets [your] competitive juice flowing.
– *Steve Ballmer*

I've even played some golf ... because everyone else in my family does. Actually, right now I'm a little addicted.

[You do] not hide [your] cutthroat instincts.
– Time, *January 13, 1997*

It cost Mike Tyson three million dollars (he forfeited ten percent of the purse) when he bit off a piece of Evander Holyfield's ear in a boxing match. Assuming that piece of ear weighed about half an ounce, you could afford to eat 592.12 pounds of Evander Holyfield if you were so inclined.

source: *Marcus, Evan. The Bill Gates Net Worth Page.*

Microriches

After the Gold Rush

Your favorite analogy: the Internet as a contemporary gold rush. A curious turn of phrase given that 1997, the year you were preparing for Microsoft's release of the next version of Windows to a capitalist market, was the centennial anniversary of gold fever in Alaska and the Yukon. In July 1897, the Klondike Gold Rush was sparked by claims of nuggets the size of a fist. Men and women – but mostly men – swarmed into northern Canada and the U.S. to get rich quick.

The analogy is quite accurate, and no-one is as optimistic about the future of the Internet as you are. You have, since the Internet started gaining popularity and attention, been directing product groups at Microsoft to make supporting the Internet a top priority.

But you almost missed it. You nearly chose the

The Internet is a gold rush. Everybody's investing in it. People feel bad if they're not involved.

In the personal computer industry, innovation is the path to success.

In 1992, the Web
didn't exist at
Microsoft or
anywhere else.
– Estrom & Eller

An Internet browser is a
trivial piece of software.
(to Wall Street analysts
in December 1995)

I want every product
plan to try and go
overboard on Internet
features. (memo to
executive Microsoft
staff, May 26, 1995)

[You are] famous for
contradicting
[your]self; unlike many
lesser tycoons [you]
would rather be right
than consistent.
– Mother Jones,
January/February 1998

wrong road and drove off-track. You almost lost your prominence when you failed to predict how quickly the Internet would grow, and how important it would become. You had instead gambled on CD-ROM technology, and when Netscape Communications threatened to completely dominate the Internet server market, you had to play catch-up. Good thing you had the money and the people to move fast. Good thing you had Windows 95 in which to freely distribute your browser software. Not so good that the federal government got involved. More on that coming up.

But you admitted that you had veered onto the wrong highway. You even revised *The Road Ahead*, your bestselling book, when it came out in paper-back. You had to add twenty percent more material to include the Internet in your future vision. Good thing you had a chance to look ahead twice.

In your *New York Times* end-of-the-year column for 1996, you went "out on a limb" to predict what was to come in 1997. Nearly every prediction dealt with the Internet. Now, with Internet Explorer firmly in place, and your content sites – MSNBC and *Slate*, for example – have made up all the ground you lost. If it wasn't for that pesky federal government.

SWIFTWATER BILL GATES

During the frenzied days of the Gold Rush in Alaska and the Canadian Yukon, one colorful yet true-life character who made a fortune was William Gates. Also known as "Swiftwater Bill." While full accounts of Swiftwater Bill's life are scarce, two prospectors, Edward B. Lung and Tappan Adney, ran into Swiftwater Bill while in Dawson City.

· · · · ·

From *Black Sand and Gold: True Alaska-Yukon Gold-Rush Story*, 1956:

"Ah, look who's coming down the trail with his gang of miners!" suddenly exclaimed Patton.

"Who?" I asked, looking up the trail with interest.

"Why, it's Swiftwater Bill Gates himself, the notorious gambler of Dawson! Has a rich claim up on the Eldorado and is also associated with Big Alex McDonald, the Klondike King. He's probably headed for Dawson to gamble away another fortune!"

Even if he hadn't been in the lead, it would have been easy to have spotted this unusual character. I stared with interest at the gambler as he quickly approached us, swinging along the trail. Swiftwater Bill presented almost a comical picture. He was a man perhaps five feet eight inches tall and he tripped along in a laughable, bowlegged fashion. On his head he wore a derby tipped jauntily over one eye, and he puffed on a long cigar, leaving a cloud of smoke trailing behind him. His complexion was swarthy; his eyes and hair were brown; and he had a thick beard of

The surging popularity of the communications network called the Internet is the most important single development in the computer industry since the IBM PC was introduced in 1981.

The rise of the Internet, [you] freely admit, caught Microsoft off-guard and now challenges its primacy.
– Salon, *December 2, 1995*

Microsoft was not the only company caught by surprise when the Internet burst into public view, and it was one of the quickest to begin a recovery.
– *James Gleick*

the same color. A loud-colored vest glorified his thick chest, and a businessman's suit of striped material covered his rather uneven figure. His pants were tucked into high, mud-covered boots, miner's style.

As he approached closer, I could see that he was literally covered with big yellow nuggets; nuggets on his stick pin, large nuggets glistened on his watch chain, and he wore several large, nuggety rings. A gold buckle studded with nuggets adorned his waist-line. As Swiftwater Bill came abreast of us, we stepped aside to let him pass. His peculiar walk slowed to a stagger.

"Hurry, fellows! Keep coming with that gold! We've got to make Dawson for that big game at Kerry's Saloon!" he called back loudly to his miners for our benefit as he brushed by us.

"Well, I'll be darned!" I said after they had passed on down the trail. "So that's Swiftwater Bill! But where did he get that name?"

"Oh, it's a big joke in Dawson about his nick-name," laughed Patton. "He boasts that he stayed for a time at Miles Canyon helping pilot some of the stampeders through those dangerous waters. But the fact of the matter is, he's scared to death of swift water! Yep, Swiftwater Bill is quite a character around Dawson!" Then he added musingly, "And he's quite a ladies' man, too! Looks up all of the pretty show girls who come to town. Right now, he's court-ing a new one. . . ."

(I heard later that he married two of the Drum-mond girls, and his third unsuccessful venture in the field of matrimony followed later when he married

---

Gold rushes tend to promote overboard behavior. People get so carried away by the prospect of instant riches that they tend to overbid for easy opportunities and ignore longer-term realities.

Microbasics Microjobs Microvisits Microvehicles Microhome
Microplay **Microriches** Micropolitics Microgiving Microfolk
Microreligion Microworries Microdreams Microimage Microman

61

one of their cousins, who nearly cleaned him out of
his fortune. Also, I heard that, on one of his trips out to
Seattle, he made the headlines of newspapers all over
the country by standing in a Seattle hotel window
and tossing bills of various denominations to the
crowds of amazed and gaping people who delighted-
ly scrambled to pick up the bills which rained down
from Swiftwater's hotel window! Occasionally, he
would wave a bill tantalizingly in the air, then he
would shock his audience by nonchalantly lighting
his cigar with it! All through these escapades, they
said, he wore a very conspicuous parka and was
adorned with his traditional number of Klondike
nuggets. It was rumored many times that he was
hooked up with a large London mining syndicate and
that he had made millions for them – and, no doubt
for himself, too! In Dawson, I was to see him many
times gambling away fortunes which would have
made the hearts of many a poor fellow glad!)

· · • · ·

After the big game, Swiftwater Bill, the notorious
gambler, came swaggering into the saloon with a fellow named Pierce. Both men seemed very drunk.
There was a pool table at the end of the room and,
while a crowd gathered around them, they began
playing. The two men at first bet $10 a game; the next
game they loudly raised to $50; then upped it to $200
for several games more; and at the end of the afternoon, they raised the final game to $500 while we all
pressed closer, watching with interest.

Swiftwater Bill was dressed almost as I had first
seen him on the Bonanza trail a week before – in his

I am a total believer in
the Internet. The
Internet is a revolution.
(May 1996)

When you're failing,
you're forced to be
creative, to dig deep
and think hard,
night and day.

striped business suit, with pants tucked into muddy boots, loud vest and a brown derby hat perched ludicrously on his head. He puffed incessantly on a long, expensive cigar, blowing thick clouds of smoke over the billiard table into the faces of his eager audience.

He had a bottle of whisky, from which he kept taking nips all afternoon. And he was finally so drunk that he could hardly hold his cue and many of his aims went amiss, the balls shooting off into the crowd. His stickpin, rings and chains of yellow gold nuggets glowed mockingly at us under the artificial light. Obviously, Swiftwater Bill enjoyed flashing his gold and being in the limelight, and played for the benefit of us gaping stampeders. There was no doubt . . . he was a born showman! Swiftwater won the $10 game, but lost all the rest. At the end of the final game, he staggered to the bar and downed several more glasses of liquor, cheering Pierce loudly as the winner, then challenging him to take him on again. But Pierce was wary. It was plain to see he was through for the day. Hadn't he won a small fortune in just one afternoon?

"Aw, that's nothin'! A thousand dollars in one afternoon is nothin' for Swiftwater Bill to lose!" said one of the bystanders. "He'll win it all back and more too, tonight in poker. Just wait and see! Trouble with Swiftwater this afternoon, he didn't have his lady love along! She seems to bring him luck. Boy, you should see her! She's a dazzler! And you should see the gold he showers her with. Five hundred dollars at a crack! No one knows how many five hundreds she's collected! But, man, oh, man! the miners say it's plenty . . . and they oughta know! Yep, she's a five-hundred-dollar-baby, if you know what I mean!"

"Fellow, be sure to come back tonight to see her and the big game," volunteered another miner. "I hear Swiftwater is gonna play Joe Hollingshead for that two hundred forty thousand dollars he just won this afternoon. I'll wager he'll get a big hunk of it, too! Boy, it'll be a show! When Swiftwater wins, he always treats the crowd. What does he care if it costs three hundred dollars a round? That's just peanuts to him! Yep, fellow, it'll be the show of your life!"

"But doesn't it seem silly, after all," I remarked, "for these fellows to get such foolish pleasure out of gambling and squandering so much gold?"

"Perhaps," replied the miner, "but the main attraction in every gold camp are always gamblin' and wimmin!"

· · • · ·

In our tent that evening, on the bank of the Yukon, only a short distance from where the dozens of big gambling games were going on, Stacey and I rolled wearily into our sleeping bags, not caring to take part in any more of the high life of Dawson. Besides, we had seen Swiftwater Bill in action several evenings before at the faro table. He had won a large fortune in gold dust, with his well-known voluptuous $500 baby looking on with calculating approval in all of her brittle, scintillating splendor!

The Internet is another case where people who are selling pans to the prospectors often will do better than the prospectors themselves.

· · • · ·

From *The Klondike Stampede*, 1899:

The aforementioned "Swiftwater Bill," whose chief claim to attention seems to have been the way he

"blew in" money and the ease with which – speaking in the vernacular of the mining-camp – his "leg could be pulled" by the fair sex, spent $40,000 and had to borrow $5000 to go outside with. His claim was good for it, though. He quarrelled with his "lady friend," and, observing her order eggs in a restaurant, he bought up every egg in town – no fewer than nine hundred in all – at a cost of $1 each. He wore his *mukluks* in the streets of San Francisco, threw money into the streets, and, in other ways ostentatiously displayed his new wealth, his vanity and craving for notoriety making him ridiculous even in Dawson.

· · · · ·

There are curious similarities between Swiftwater Bill and yourself. Like Swiftwater Bill, for instance, you have more money than you know what to do with. And, as you have been accused of buying things so no one else can have them, so did Swiftwater Bill buy every egg in Dawson City. When he learned he had a rival for the affections of Gussie Lamore, she with the penchant for eggs, buying up all the eggs was the only course of action that would effectively stymie his rival.

But similarities aside, what is the relationship between you and Swiftwater Bill? You've never mentioned him publicly, but that doesn't mean anything. Some journalists think he was your great-great-grandfather. For others, the blood relationship is less important than the obvious parallels. Terrence Cole, a professor of history at the University of Alaska, Fairbanks, knows the truth.

"Swiftwater Bill Gates was a notorious liar," says

[You are] the consummate opportunist.
– Fortune, *May 26, 1997*

When you have a gold rush, everybody thinks, "Oh I'll do a whatever service." It's pretty tough to succeed, though.

Microbasics Microjobs Microvisits Microvehicles Microhome
Microplay **Microriches** Micropolitics Microgiving Microfolk
Microreligion Microworries Microdreams Microimage Microman

65

Dr. Cole. "A storyteller." The legends about him, though, are grounded in reality. Dr. Cole says Swiftwater Bill worked hard to create his own legend, and while he allegedly struck it rich a number of times, it may not have been as often as he claimed. We do know that Swiftwater Bill was married at least six times, went bankrupt after the seventh, and moved to Peru around 1915.

"There is no substance to the story that Microsoft's Bill Gates is related to Swiftwater Bill Gates," chuckles Dr. Cole. "It's a freshman course in cause-and-effect." And yet, the similarities are so pronounced. As Swiftwater Bill had his gold rush, you have yours: the Internet.

If you were Bill Gates you would not be related to Swiftwater Bill Gates, whose real name was Goetze. But according to Terrence Cole, history professor at the University of Alaska, if Swiftwater Bill were alive today, he would say you were related.

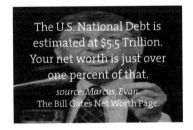

The U.S. National Debt is estimated at $5.5 Trillion. Your net worth is just over one percent of that.
source: Marcus, Evan.
The Bill Gates Net Worth Page.

Micropolitics

Life on Capitol Hill

You had an early political career as a page in the Washington State Capitol in Olympia and also in Washington, D.C. The politicians and the high-rolling businessmen must have been role-models for you, adding to your sense of wonder about what it might be like to wield such power. You must have seen them reading *Fortune*, then started reading it yourself, hoping that in some way, reading that magazine would help you achieve what you always wanted.

But your early experiences in the political arena must have been forgotten, or you were too innocent to perceive how important it is to schmooze the right people, grease the right palms. Insiders speculate that one of the reasons the Federal Trade Commission and the Department of Justice were able to continue with their investigations for so long is because neither you nor Microsoft had any lobbying presence in Washington, D.C. That's changed now.

I expect to be able to vote from my PC.
(on politics via the Internet)

I think it's fair to say that [in terms of] contributing to political causes and involvement in Washington, D.C., I am – or at least was – naïve.

If you were Bill Gates you wouldn't say much in public about your political leanings. At one event you mentioned you were a Democrat and for a while after that's all anyone talked about. Now you just won't say one way or another. One thing that you make very clear is that your political views are separate from Microsoft's.

Can you be both? Why not? When it comes to business you could be a Republican, and with social issues you could be a Democrat. Model for the future, that's you.

The politicians don't know what side they're on, either. Some know enough to be supportive, but others just can't help but take a swing. In early May 1998, two U.S. senators had it out over the impact of your company.

One senator, the Mudslinger, warned that Microsoft's business dealings were making computer companies and consumers "increasingly beholden to Microsoft for software products." The Mudslinger suggested that a marketing strategy for the release of Windows 98 would be to make arrangements with the Rolling Stones again, and secure the rights to their song, "Under My Thumb."

Later on another senator, the Supporter, retaliated on your behalf, offering the Stones song "Satisfaction" as a Microsoft theme-song suggestion, arguing that Microsoft had been "satisfying customers for twenty years." The Supporter scorned those who would come

> Microsoft was naïve in not realizing the competitors were hiring lobbyists [to solicit support in Washington, D.C.].

> [You have] managed to keep an extraordinarily low political profile.
> – Mother Jones, *January/February 1998*

> Though [you] vaguely consider [yourself] a Democrat, [you] stayed neutral in the presidential election.
> – Time, *January 13, 1997*

Windows 95 rolled onto (and over) the market to the sounds of The Rolling Stones' "Start Me Up."

between Microsoft and their customers, letting them know that "You can't always get what you want."

And while you and Microsoft didn't know much about the political game when you first started rolling along, you have learned quick lessons, having now aligned yourselves with certain lobbying groups and individuals who know where the influence lies, and how best to pay for that all-important political support.

You've always learned quickly and this is no exception. You passed your final exam with flying colors. The Department of Justice just may back off after all.

Every politician wants to be associated with the future. *(on why politicians want to be seen talking to you)*

It makes perfect sense for politicians to be interested in productive new technology. No leader wants his or her country to fall behind.

MICROMAN AS A PUBLIC COMPANY		
RANK	COMPANY	1995 GDP
1	GM	$178.17 Billion
2	Ford	$153.63 Billion
3	Exxon	$122.38 Billion
6	IBM	$78.51 Billion
7	Chrysler	$61.15 Billion
8	Mobil	$59.98 Billion
	MICROMAN	$56.85 Billion
9	Philip Morris	$56.11 Billion
10	AT&T	$53.26 Billion
11	Boeing	$45.8 Billion
137	Microsoft	$11.36 Billion

source: *Marcus, Evan. The Bill Gates Net Worth Page.*

In the future, direct democracy will be feasible. But personally I think representative democracy is better. In the future, we'll have to choose representative democracy not because it's the only system available but because we believe that it's the best approach available.

Microgiving

Philanthropist Extraordinaire

They say that money is only as good as the paper it's printed on, and your net worth is not even that good. It exists as some ethereal number in cyberspace. Knowing full well that you have more money than you could ever spend, you have pledged to, one day, give it all away.

Aside from a small stipend for your children – just enough to be comfortable – you've promised to donate ninety-five percent of your fortune to charitable causes and scientific endeavours, with a focus on education, population issues, and access to technology.

Your first major donation since becoming a self-made millionaire occured in 1986, when you and your friend Paul Allen gave $2.2 million to your high school, Lakeside School, to be used to build a new science and mathematics building. That building is called "Allen-Gates Hall."

Playboy: Does your net worth of multi-billions … boggle your mind?

Microman: It's a ridiculous number. But remember, 95 percent of it I'm just going to give away.

Ten years later, the size of your donations expanded to $27 million, including $15 million to Harvard even though you never finished your junior year. Imagine what you might have given them if you'd finished your degree! Your friend and Microsoft executive vice-president Steve Ballmer also gave $10 million to Harvard. The money will help build and maintain the Maxwell Dworkin building (named after your mothers) to house electrical engineering, computing, and communications and will also pay for one professor.

You've given $6 million to Stanford and $34 million to the University of Washington, which will be used, in part, for genetic research. Another $2 million that was earmarked for UW will help build a new law school building, to be named for your father, William

> The biggest negative we [the U.S.] have is that our education system isn't as good as it needs to be.

> Compared to almost anything else in a developed society, the cost of investment in education is low – and the returns are high.

> I don't own dollars. I own Microsoft stock.

> If scientists were to identify the exact location of one tiny piece of genetic information per second, 24 hours a day every day, it would take a century to map all 3 billion of them.

If you wanted to spend all of your money within twelve years, and you worked hard at achieving this task by spending twenty-four hours a day, 365 days a year, you would have to spend:

$4.74 Billion per year
$394.8 Million per month
$90.79 Million per week
$12.97 Million every day
$540.5 Thousand every hour
$9 Thousand a minute
$150 every second of every hour of every day for eleven years

source: Marcus, Evan. The Bill Gates Net Worth Page.

Microbasics Microjobs Microvisits Microvehicles Microhome
Microplay Microriches Micropolitics **Microgiving** Microfolk
Microreligion Microworries Microdreams Microimage Microman

73

H. Gates. Isn't it nice that it's also going to be named after you?

As your wealth grows larger, faster, you are giving more of it away. In their review of the "Most Generous Americans" of 1997, *Fortune* placed you number 4 because of your two major contributions to education: $10 million to Lakeside School, and $200 million to form the Gates Library Foundation (*www.glf.com*), which will ensure Internet access for public libraries in the United States and Canada. The first round of grants were announced on February 24, 1998 and many of them are supporting programs in Alabama.

Of course, these are only the donations in North America. You're also giving money to support educational projects in the rest of the world, including 12 million pounds ($19.2 million U.S.) to Cambridge University.

The truth is, you have so much money that you need help giving it all away. You have put into a foundation a total of $200 million since 1992. Your father

> The same libraries that serve communities with books … can also serve the computing and electronic-information needs of citizens.

> Giving is a complex thing. You have to find things you really believe in and that are fun to give to.

HANDING IT OUT

According to the National Coalition for the Homeless, there are 760,000 homeless people in the United States. You could give each of them $78,804.10.

According to Save the Children, it costs $250 to sponsor one child for a year. This means you could provide for 236.88 Million children for a year.

It costs roughly $30,000 to purchase the supplies to build a three bedroom house for Habitat for Humanities. You could provide supplies for nearly two million homes. Assuming 4.5 occupants per house, you would be housing 8,527,667 people.

source: Marcus, Evan. The Bill Gates Net Worth Page.

Your royalties from your 1995 book *The Road Ahead*, are being donated to a non-profit fund. Administered by the National Foundation for Improvement in Education the money will be used to provide support for educators who are working towards having computers in classrooms. *The Road Ahead* was on the *New York Times* bestseller list for eighteen weeks, held the number one position for seven of them, and has sold millions of copies.

administers the foundation, donating the money to education, population control, and the United Way (kind of a legacy for your mother, perhaps, who was a strong supporter of the United Way, and for a time sat on its national board).

But why, oh why, do you want to rid yourself of all this hard-earned money? Do you feel guilty about having more money than anyone can possibly conceive of, more than you and your extended family could ever spend? If you were Bill Gates, time is money. Maybe you'll find a way to buy time.

SHARING WITH
HUMANKIND

The estimated population of the United States: 270.02 Million. You could give $210.54 to every person in the United States. The estimated population of Earth: 5.93 Billion. You could give $9.59 to every person on the entire planet and still have fifteen million dollars left over for incidentals.

source: Marcus, Evan. The Bill Gates Net Worth Page.

Microfolk

The Inner Circle, The Outer Threat

FAMILY

If you were Bill Gates you would have been born of Mary and William Henry Gates Senior. You would have two sisters: Kristi, a year older than you, and Libby, nine years younger. Your nuclear family calls you "Trey," because you are the third William Henry Gates in the family tree. Besides, it avoids a great deal of confusion that would have led from you and your father sharing a name.

Your mother, Mary Maxwell, was born in Seattle in 1929. A banker's daughter, she grew up in the social environment of prominent families. "She was a star at social intercourse," your father told a *Time* reporter. A teacher and regent at the University of Washington, Mary was gracious with her time, serving on boards at the University of Washington, USWest, and First

Privacy is a very interesting issue. I think people are a little naive about how much data exist about them electronically today.

Interstate Bancorp. She also understood the importance of charity and served on the United Way's
national board. After she died in 1994, the City of Seattle named a street after her.

You are a lot like your mother. She, too, was confident, determined, intelligent, and competitive. When
describing the bridge games she used to organize,
your father said: "The play was quite serious. Winning mattered." Your similarities caused some fric-
tion, though. When you were a pre-teen you had dif-
ferences in opinion with your mother. She wanted
you to do what you were told. You had different
ideas. In the battle of wills between you and her, you
won. "She came around to accepting that it was futile
trying to compete with [you]," said your father.

Your father, born in Bremerton, Washington, is a
retired lawyer who still lives in the house you grew
up in. You still employ the law firm your father
worked for and you have him running one of your
philanthropic foundations. Although you are so busy
you don't see your father much, you do communicate
regularly by e-mail. He remarried. His new wife,
Mimi, is the director of the Seattle Art Museum.

Your sister Kristi is a tax accountant (she works for
you). Libby is raising two children. You don't see them
much, either, but you still spend holidays together.

Microbasics Microjobs Microvisits Microvehicles Microhome
Microplay Microriches Micropolitics Microgiving **Microfolk**
Microreligion Microworries Microdreams Microimage Microman

77

FAMOUS PEOPLE SEEN WITH MICROMAN
Do you call them by their first names?

Mick Jagger	head Stone
Nelson Mandela	South African politician
Steve Jobs	Apple-man
Steve Wozniak	ex-Apple-man
Shaquille O'Neal	basketball player, *Shazaam*
H.D. Deve Gowda	Indian politician
Rudolph Giuliani	New York City politician
Kofi Annan	secretary-general of the United Nations
Jane Pauley	journalist, ex-*Today*
Warren Buffett	rich guy
Ruth Cardoso	Brazilian politician
Ted Turner	another rich guy, owns stuff like CNN and the Atlanta Braves
Larry King	journalist, as in *Live With* on CNN
Connie Chung	journalist, ex-anchor
B. Netanyahu	Israeli politician
Andrew Grove	Intel pal
Bill Clinton	U.S. Prez
Glen Campbell	singer, songwriter, *Rhinestone Cowboy*
Tom Brokaw	journalist, NBC anchor
Jacques Chirac	French politician
Barbra Streisand	singer, actor, *Yentl*
Tony Blair	United Kingdom politician
Newt Gingrich	U.S. politician
Dolly Parton	singer, actor, only works *9 to 5*
Reba McEntire	Windows 98 spokesmodel
V. Chernomyrdin	Russian politician
Jiang Zemin	Chinese politician
Rupert Murdoch	20th-Century Fox, newspaper baron, another rich guy
Michael Ovitz	agent, ex-Creative Artists Agency, ex-Disney
Kevin Costner	actor, director, *Wolves*-man, *Postman*
Steven Spielberg	director, producer, extra-terrestrial *Hook*
David Geffen	music magnate, also rich
Jeffrey Katzenberg	ex-Disney
Willie Nelson	singer, songwriter, *Outlaw*
Jay Leno	Windows 95 spokesmodel
Michael Crichton	writer, dinosaur

FRIENDS

Your best friend in grade nine was Kent Evans. You remember reading *Fortune* with him, dreaming about conquering the world. Kent got involved in computers as you did, but had problems dealing with the pressures of working so hard at such a young age. He took up mountain climbing, a natural hobby for someone who had grown up surrounded by mountains.

I had never thought of people dying. At the service, I was supposed to speak, but I couldn't get up. For two weeks I couldn't do anything at all. *(on your reaction to Kent's death)*

Kent's death in a climbing fall while you were in high school must have been your first tangible evidence of mortality. Did you delve more deeply into computers, a way to deal with your grief? Were you spending more time thinking about the future, about how life could be – would be – different?

Your other friend – with whom you learned BASIC from a manual – was Paul Allen. As part of the Lakeside Programmers Group at Lakeside School you and he started programming the teletype computer terminal the Mothers' Club had donated. At times tempers flared.

Okay, but I'm in charge, and I'll get used to being in charge, and it'll be hard to deal with me from now on unless I'm in charge. *(after you agreed to return to the Lakeside Programmers Group)*

You and Paul had power struggles, about who was going to lead, who would follow, who would have control. Paul was older, by three years, and felt that he should be president. Once, when he wasn't sure there was enough work for the four people in the group, you were excused. Then Paul realized he needed you to write code, and you ended up in charge.

Kent's death seemed to bring you and Paul closer together. When you left for Harvard, Paul followed.

At Microsoft the arguments that happened when you and Paul were in school continued to rage. Your

Microbasics Microjobs Microvisits Microvehicles Microhome
Microplay Microriches Micropolitics Microgiving **Microfolk**
Microreligion Microworries Microdreams Microimage Microman

79

tendency to spark dialogue by bullying people was having an effect on your friendship. Did Paul have a problem with your aggressive, argumentative nature?

Paul decided to leave the company in 1983 when he was diagnosed with Hodgkins disease. Your friendship may have suffered during the growth of Microsoft, but today you are friends. Allen owns the Portland Trail Blazers, Ticketmaster, a big part of America Online, and his own airplane. He is also on the Microsoft board. You convinced him to come back.

In 1978, a Japanese college student and computer enthusiast called you wanting to work with Microsoft. Kazuhiko Nishi – you called him Kay – and you were the same age, into the same things. By 1979, Kay was, as Microsoft's exclusive distributor in East Asia, responsible for nearly half of Microsoft's business. Comfortable in both Japanese and North American cultures, Kay helped make a name for Microsoft in the countries that were becoming increasingly important in technological development. You

We were true partners. (*on your relationship with Paul*)

[You] bring to the company the idea that conflict can be a good thing.... [You] know it's important to avoid that gentle civility that keeps you from getting to the heart of an issue quickly.
– *Steve Ballmer*

LAYING DOLLAR BILLS END TO END

If you converted your net worth to dollar bills you would need more dollar bills than there are in the United States. But if you could, and you laid those dollar bills end to end, you would have a line of bills that would stretch 5.5 Million miles. Laying dollar bills end to end, twenty-four hours a day, at the rate of two bills per second, would take you 901.36 years. But you could travel:
• from Seattle to New York and back 945.9 times
• to the moon and back 11.5 times

source: Marcus, Evan. The Bill Gates Net Worth Page.

[You] have an emotional loyalty to a few old friends.
– Time, *January 13, 1997*

described him as "flamboyant," but knew that his flashy presentation got the attention you all wanted. Kay no longer works with Microsoft. He took his company in a different direction than you wanted for Microsoft. You insist the two of you are still friends.

Although you weren't at Harvard for very long, you met a few people, perhaps the most important of whom was Steve Ballmer. He is a sports guy who managed the football team at Harvard and actually finished his degree. You brought him to Microsoft as an equity partner in 1980 to help with sales and marketing. He has taken the analogy of business as a sport to the extreme. He overflows with energy, gives pep talks, gets employees "pumped-up." It doesn't always work with a bunch of programmers who were ridiculed and even beat-up by football players and simply can't relate to him.

You argue with him too but don't have to worry about him flipping out and popping you in the nose. He is too much in awe of you. And you rewarded him for his efforts at Microsoft by naming him president on July 21, 1998.

In those early days, at Harvard and at Microsoft, you and Steve did bachelor things together; he was your link to a more social existence. If it wasn't for Steve you might still be spending all your time at the computer or solving a puzzle. He was the guy who would get you involved in late-night poker games in the dorms, invited you to join a college eating club, guided you on jaunts to New York City. Was he the guy who introduced you to the Combat Zone – Cam-

Like every great salesman, Ballmer could charge into meetings and immediately raise the crowd's temperature with his booming voice. He infused a contagious energy, and many developers thrived on this "mission from God" intensity.
– Edstrom & Eller

Within three weeks of Steve's arrival at Microsoft, we had the first of our very few arguments.

Ballmer's modus operandi for dealing with technical issues was to pound on the developers until they caved in.
– Edstrom & Eller

Microbasics Microjobs Microvisits Microvehicles Microhome
Microplay Microriches Micropolitics Microgiving **Microfolk**
Microreligion Microworries Microdreams Microimage Microman

81

bridge's red-light district? Was he around when you took that hit of LSD that tripped you into hallucinating that the corner of a table was going to stab you in the eye?

When you want to brainstorm ideas and zip from one topic to another with blinding speed you call Nathan Myhrvold, who runs Microsoft's advance-research group. He's got a Ph.D. in physics from Princeton and worked with Stephen Hawking at Cambridge University. He's also a part-time chef. When the two of you start talking, building on one another's ideas, everyone else steps back to watch, to listen.

Warren Buffett is an investor and one of America's richest men (what did it feel like when you passed him on the list of Richest Americans?). He is older than you, old enough to be your father, but you are friends nonetheless. Was he a role model for you? You've never exploited your friendship with Warren financially – he only bought one hundred shares of Microsoft when you first met, as a curiosity – and now you don't need to. You take vacations together, play bridge together. Unlike you, Warren plans to give all his money away after he dies. He wants it to be used to study and control population.

Warren doesn't invest in technology, so the chances of you two working closely together aren't likely unless you join forces and head for the media/content companies. Buying television and cable networks might be just up your respective alleys. Together you take positions one and two on the *Forbes* list of the world's richest individuals. Buying up the world can't be that hard to do.

> I work at the *Tonight Show*, owned by NBC which stands for "Now Bill Compatible." – *Jay Leno, at the Windows 95 launch*

> Talking to Myhrvold was a little like smoking dope. It could give you "insights," but in the light of day those insights often didn't make any sense.
> – *Edstrom & Eller*

FEMALES

In 1984, you met Ann Winblad, a "software entrepreneur and venture capitalist." The two of you, although living in different cities, started dating. Your "virtual dates" involved seeing the same movie at the same time, albeit in different cities, then discussing the film on your cellular phones afterwards. She turned you into a vegetarian for a while. While vacationing together you studied biotechnology, physics, and evolution. While the two of you broke up in 1987, you remain good friends. You even asked for her approval before proposing marriage to Melinda.

I like to learn.

You met Melinda French, born in 1965 and raised Catholic in Dallas, at a Microsoft event in 1987. Melinda was a product and general manager with Microsoft, working with the multimedia department, helping to develop Encarta and Cinemania. She also worked on Word, Works, and Publisher, and was general manager of information products when she retired from Microsoft in 1994.

We have to pay particular attention to correcting the gender imbalance. *(on future technological developers)*

She retired because, while she may not have needed to work before, she certainly didn't have to now. She became your wife, you her husband. The two of you met in 1987, but it would be six years before you proposed marriage. The two of you were returning to Seattle from Palm Springs. You quietly had the pilot alter course and instead landed in Omaha, where your friend Warren Buffett was waiting. He took you and Melinda to a jewelry store that he had arranged to be open where you and Melinda selected a ring.

Certainly a few romances around Microsoft have benefitted from e-mail. When Melinda and I were first going out, we took advantage of it.

You and Melinda were married on January 1, 1994

in Lanai, Hawaii. You rented every helicopter in the area to ensure there would be no interruptions by paparazzi during the ceremony. Steve Ballmer was your best man. Willie Nelson sang at the reception.

Now Melinda is on the board of trustees at Duke University, where she earned her two degrees – in computer science and business – and spends time working with charitable organizations. And raising Jennifer.

In Seattle, Washington, at just after 6 p.m. on April 26, 1996, your eight-pound, six-ounce daughter was born. You and Melinda giver her the name Jennifer Katharine. Now you have a family of your own. You are the father of an actual living, breathing being named Jennifer, not just an entity called Microsoft. But you seem to be taking to fatherhood the way you took to computers: with fascination. Even new innovations in the realm of diapers intrigue you.

And while you thought that children were kind of

> There's some magic [between you and Melinda] that's hard to describe.

> Married life is a simpler life. Who I spend my time with is established in advance.

STACKING BILLS

Now that you've converted your net worth to dollar bills and if you could actually balance them in a stack, that stack would be over twenty million feet, or 3,850 miles high. What if you decided to keep all that cash under your mattress? Let's assume that you and Melinda sleep on a king size mattress, which has an area of 43 1/3 square feet. It takes 397.57 dollar bills to cover a king size mattress . Using all your money you could cover the mattress with bills 142,996,178 bills deep. That means you would have a jump of 613,718 inches or 9.68 miles to get from the bed to the floor each morning.

source: Marcus, Evan. The Bill Gates Net Worth Page.

> There's some competitive tension.... It's a very healthy thing. *(on life at Microsoft)*

boring until they were able to talk, you're quite taken with your daughter. But despite having so much money, you insist that your children will not be spoiled by having enormous sums at their disposal. You say you will set aside ten million dollars for each of your children. The rest will be up to them.

FREAKS & FOES

If you have any enemies, they have become so because of work; because of the way you do business. Not everyone can appreciate how committed you are to your vision. Competitors in the technology and software industries love to hate you. Some of them get lots of publicity and media attention because their animosity toward you is so intense.

But for every person you have fallen out of favour with, there are many you have won back: Paul Allen and Steve Jobs are only two of many. You have a way of working through problems with friends. Maybe it's because they end up agreeing with you in the end.

Nobody can accurately speculate on the motives behind the many groups and individuals on the Internet who openly protest you and your actions. Some of them are die-hard Apple fanatics, others are concerned – and their concern may be justified – that you and your business interests are reaching a point where you will be unstoppable. Attitudes range from caution to outright rage.

The most dangerous person to you and your empire is Joel I. Klein. He seems harmless enough in the Department of Justice's employee photo, but as

At home we have this thing, a special diaper pail, that if the diaper doesn't smell good you just put it in and twist it around and there's no odor.

I don't believe in burdening any children I might have with that. They'll have enough. They'll be comfortable.... The point is that ridiculous sums of money can be confusing.

If [my competitors] really think I'm going to work a lot less just because I'm married, that's an error.

Microbasics Microjobs Microvisits Microvehicles Microhome
Microplay Microriches Micropolitics Microgiving **Microfolk**
Microreligion Microworries Microdreams Microimage Microman

85

MICROMAN-HATING WEBSITES IN NUMEROUS
LANGUAGES AND BASED AROUND THE WORLD

www.enemy.org · Micro$oft Hate Page

www.microshaft.com

www.wwwebmistress.com/msnot · Msnot: the official MSN2 hate
site

www.lightman.co.uk/windoesnot · Windoesnot 95

www.jwp.bc.ca/saulm/ii/ms.htm · Microsoff

members.tripod.com/~antiMicrosoft · The antiMicrosoft (UK) Website

www.stale.com · Stale

members.tripod.com/~megasloth · Megasloth

www.successmarketplace.com/shops/spoggesticker/index.html ·
SPOGGE: Society for the Prevention of Gates Getting Everything

www.jas.com/ms-shame.shtml · The William Gates Wall of Shame

klbproductions.com/yogi/stop_microsoft · Stop Microsoft

www.vcnet.com.bms · The Monopoly Clock: Boycott Micro$oft

come.to/ie-hate · Internet Explorer Hatepage

www.geocities.com/CapitolHill/1450/WebRing.htm

pages.nyu.edu/~ntc4296/winblows.html · Winblows95

thunder.indstate.edu/~hunters · Why Windows 95 Sucks

members.tripod.com/~micropap · MicroPap Corporation

www.tcp.ca/gsb/PC/Win95-subliminals.htm · Subliminal Messages
in Windows 95

www.personal.engin.umich.edu/~athaler.microsuck.html · The
Microsuck Hate Page

hum.auc.dk/~trekan/antims/Anti-MS_homepage.html · The Official Anti-Microsoft Homepage

vidalia.unh.edu/~black/cgi-bin/dartMap · Throw Darts at Bill Gates

www.wirehub.nl/~wizzie/SAIE.html

www.progsoc.uts.edu.au/~baitoven/hatems/index.html · I Hate
Microsoft

www.chernigob.ua/hate · M$ Haters Club – Russia

www.algonet.se/~jkumlin/antims/page1.html · The Bill Gates Love-
center

www.mlink.net/~vandry/microsoft.html · No Microsoft

users.aol.com/machcu/amsa.html

www.geocities.com/sunsetstrip/club/7666 · Grupo Anti-Microsoft
Brazil

microsuxx.home.ml.org · Microsuxx

[You are] not threat-
ened by smart peo-
ple, only stupid ones.
– *Nathan Myhrvold*

Go ahead and hate
Microman, if you
want. But hate him
for the right reasons.
. . . Hate Microman
because he can't
help himself. He
must squash his
rivals, intimidate his
allies, and treat his
customers with a
mixture of affection
and resentment.
– Mother Jones,
*January/February
1998*

the Assistant Attorney General in charge of the Antitrust Division, Joel really is your nemesis. He's practiced law for more than twenty years, was an advisor to President Clinton (the "other" Bill), and has now dedicated his career to breaking Microsoft. He's as determined as you are to "crush" the opposition.

You and Klein are both Harvard alumni. In fact, he graduated from law school in Cambridge just before you arrived as an undergraduate. You may have seen each other across the quad at one time.

Maybe it's a generational thing and those fifty-somethings just don't understand what you are doing.

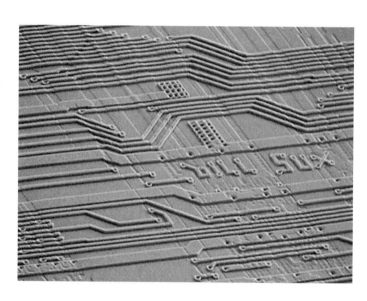

HI-TECH GRAFFITI A scanning electron microscope picture of the latest Intel Pentium chip used in the manufacture of tens of thousands of PCs reveals the opinions of two Intel engineers. The engineers have since been fired.

Microreligion

Spreading the Gospel

You have no publicly-stated religious affiliation. Your family was Congregationalist but you do not practice it and haven't for some time.

Melinda, a Catholic, plans to baptize your daughter, Jennifer. The deal was that if you started going to church, Jennifer could be raised by whatever religion you wanted. But you just can't bring yourself to give up your Sundays. Someday Jennifer will make her own decisions about it all, anyway.

None of it really matters. You have become what amounts to a religious figure yourself. It started back in the early days when the Altair, the first personal computer, was being used exclusively by enthusiasts. You knew, even at that young age, that your passion for computers was contagious. During your cross-country road trip to start computer clubs you passed your excitement to club members, who in turn passed it to the unsuspecting curious.

I don't have any evidence on that. *(on whether there is something special about the human soul)*

Just in terms of allocation of time resource, religion is not very efficient. There's a lot more I could be doing on a Sunday morning.

Your cult of personality was fresh and new. It heralded a bright, productive, and exciting future. That future is something that you are helping to make happen, and you are making sure that the world knows the path to enlightenment will be revealed through Microsoft.

Even though I am not religious, the amazement and wonder I have about the human mind is closer to religious awe than dispassionate analysis.

But you don't see yourself in that light. You walk the streets of New York, Chicago, San Francisco, Los Angeles, without any attendants, bodyguards or otherwise. You really think of yourself as just another American citizen, working hard to make a living and not get caught eating that grape while shopping for groceries.

[You] devote about a quarter of [your] time each year to "evangelism" – that's Bill-speak for hitting the road to preach the Microsoft gospel.
– Fortune, *May 26, 1997*

WINDOWS 98

On June 25, 1998, you attended and spoke at an important sermon. That was the day that Windows 98 – the next stage of your operating system vision – hit the shelves of computer stores, bookstores, office supply stores, and any other retail outlet that was able to get stock. That evening you attended the official product launch in San Francisco. The theme of the evening was taken from *the* road-trip song, "Route 66," signifying not only your "road ahead," but a subtle jab at the Department of Justice and other competitor nay-sayers. They were eating your dust as they watched you shrink to a speck on the horizon, zooming into the distance on your Harley.

We actually spend a lot of money on evangelization.

Windows 98 is just the beginning.

The audience was made up of people from around the world. Some were connected live via closed-circuit (set up at retail stores, movie theatres, and South

Microbasics Microjobs Microvisits Microvehicles Microhome
Microplay Microriches Micropolitics Microgiving Microfolk
Microreligion Microworries Microdreams Microimage Microman

89

Africa), others were watching on the Internet. The presentation to the audience was a mixture of evangelization, demonstrations, and testimonials.

You knew that no product release could ever come close to achieving what the Windows 95 campaign accomplished. But you needed to convince consumers that this truck stop on the map that would take them from the original Windows through to your final vision, whatever it ends up being, was worth pulling into. At the Windows 98 launch there were no Jay Leno's, no Rolling Stones. Instead you had, as your special guests, everyday, average Americans. And Reba McEntire.

Reba described on video how important Windows 98 was for her to do business, keep in touch, and connect with fans. The everyday Americans – from Chicago, St. Louis, Des Moines, Arizona – were made up of seniors and students and an ex-cop who had been injured in the line of duty. They had all received advance copies of the new operating system and were raving about the superiority of Windows 98 compared to Windows 95.

There's something magical about the open road.
– *Brad Chase, Microsoft VP, at the Windows 98 product launch*

We think there are some incredible parallels between what the auto industry did, and what the PC industry is just at the beginning of doing.

One of the nice things about Windows is it's a world-wide phenomenon.
– *Brad Chase, Microsoft VP, at the Windows 98 product launch*

According to *Financial World* magazine, the total value (in 1996) of all the professional teams in all four major U.S. leagues was $16.5 Billion. That's only twenty-nine percent of your fortune.

source: Marcus, Evan. The Bill Gates Net Worth Page.

Microworries

From Pirates to Projectiles

PIRACY

If you were Bill Gates we wouldn't know much about your first major concerns. You likely experienced the same anxieties that all children and adolescents do – ghosts in the attic, skeletons in the closet, monsters under the bed – but by the time you are nineteen you are facing a much more adult problem, one that could have threatened the growth of your fortune, your empire. Piracy of software, which prevents software programmers and publishers from being paid for their work, was a paramount concern for a company who was positioning itself to be a major software producer. In early 1976 you wrote "An Open Letter to Hobbyists," which established your position on the matter.

AN OPEN LETTER TO HOBBYISTS

To me, the most critical thing in the hobby market right now is the lack of good software courses, books and software itself. Without good software and an owner who understands programming, a hobby computer is wasted. Will quality software be written for the hobby market?

Almost a year ago, Paul Allen and myself, expecting the hobby market to expand, hired Monte Davidoff and developed Altair BASIC. Though the initial work took only two months, the three of us have spent most of the last year documenting, improving and adding features to BASIC. Now we have 4K, 8K, EXTENDED, ROM and DISK BASIC. The value of the computer time we have used exceeds $40,000.

The feedback we have gotten from the hundreds of people who say they are using BASIC has all been positive. Two surprising things are apparent, however. 1) Most of these "users" never bought BASIC (less than 10% of all Altair owners have bought BASIC), and 2) The amount of royalties we have received from sales to hobbyists makes the time spent on Altair BASIC worth less than $2 an hour.

Why is this? As the majority of hobbyists must be aware, most of you steal your software. Hardware must be paid for, but software is something to share. Who cares if the people who worked on it get paid?

Is this fair? One thing you don't do by stealing software is get back at MITS for some problem you may have had. MITS doesn't make money selling software. The royalty paid to us for the manual, the tape and the overhead make it a break-even operation. One thing you do is prevent good software from being written. Who can afford to do professional work for nothing? What hobbyist can put 2-man years into programming, finding all bugs, documenting his product and distribute for free? The fact is, no one besides us has invested a lot of money in hobby software. We have written 6800 BASIC, and are writing 8080 APL and 6800 APL, but there is very little incentive to make this software available to hobbyists. Most directly, the thing you do is theft.

Microbasics Microjobs Microvisits Microvehicles Microhome
Microplay Microriches Micropolitics Microgiving Microfolk
Microreligion **Microworries** Microdreams Microimage Microman

93

What about the guys who re-sell Altair BASIC, aren't they making money on hobby software? Yes, but those who have been reported to us may lose in the end. They are the ones who give hobbyists a bad name, and should be kicked out of any club meeting they show up at.

I would appreciate letters from any one who wants to pay up, or has a suggestion or comment. Just write me at 1180 Alvarado SE, #114, Albuquerque, New Mexico, 87108. Nothing would please me more than being able to hire ten programmers and deluge the hobby market with good software.

Bill Gates
General Partner, Micro-Soft

The trend on piracy is positive. *(1996)*

You aren't quite as concerned about piracy as you once were. These days you can use the market power of Microsoft to deal with it quite simply. Rumors flying across the Internet in the days leading up to the release of Windows 98 suggested that a special program had been inserted into the new software. A program which would send a message to you if there was any pirated software on any computer, so you and Microsoft could collect what was coming to you. With many computers either connected or soon to be connected to the Internet, this is a simple task. And even if it's not true it will make people and companies and countries think twice. One hell of a rumor, that one.

[You] will need to be even more visionary and nimble than [you have] been in the past if Microsoft is to stay on top of the quickly evolving market for new computer products.

– Maclean's,
May 11, 1992

There are many, many articles that say Microsoft is about to fail. Those two extremes are silly beyond belief. We won't fail tomorrow, and we don't have a guaranteed future. That's just logical.

Everyone close to the process knew what a fluke the Windows 3.0 success had been....
The Federal Trade Commission thought the conspiracy theory held a lot more water than the fluke theory.

– Edstrom & Eller

THE FEDERAL GOVERNMENT

In 1991, not only was your Microsoft the leading supplier of operating systems for computers (at that time it was MS-DOS – Windows was just an enhancement), but you were also the primary vendor of applications software. Although you were mainly designing and producing software for Apple back in 1991, you were making the industry nervous. CEOs of other software companies seemed to think it was only a matter of time before you had the IBM-compatible market in your pocket, too.

The Federal Trade Commission had earlier perked up its ears and, in 1990, decided to investigate the chances of Microsoft developing a monopoly in the software industry. The big concern was that, with MS-DOS as the industry standard (and Windows becoming increasingly prominent), you had an inside track on producing software that would work properly.

At the same time, you were inviting any and all software developers to your Redmond headquarters to let them know exactly what could be expected in future revisions of the operating system. You wanted to make sure that they had the opportunity to revise their software accordingly. You knew that the more programs being produced to run on your operating system, the more entrenched your operating system would be. You'd win either way.

So what, exactly, you wanted to know, was the FTC so worried about?

They, obviously, weren't sure what was bothering

Microbasics Microjobs Microvisits Microvehicles Microhome
Microplay Microriches Micropolitics Microgiving Microfolk
Microreligion **Microworries** Microdreams Microimage Microman

95

them, because they let the whole thing drop without issuing a complaint. They left you alone for a while. Until, in 1993, the Department of Justice (DOJ) picked up where the FTC left off.

Joel Klein, your nemesis, leads any and all DOJ investigations into business dealings in the United States, and his time since 1993 has been devoted almost exclusively to Microsoft.

The DOJ began by looking at the same question the FTC was trying to answer: to what extent was Microsoft trying to leverage its position in the software industry as a provider of an operating system to gain control of other realms of the software industry? It is an anti-competition issue that revolves around – surprise, surprise – the Internet. The idea is that Microsoft, by distributing software (like Internet Explorer) with its operating system, is getting people to buy Microsoft products that may not have sold if they were simply on the shelf beside other similar programs (like Netscape). So, by providing Explorer for free, the argument goes, Microsoft is unfairly taking business away from Netscape, who need to sell their browser to stay in business.

The reason Microsoft can do this is because of the huge financial and people resources available to it. You and your company can afford to give away programs until a competitor goes out of business. Or you can simply buy them. Problem solved.

But when the DOJ got involved, the rules seemed to change. They blocked you from buying Intuit, the company that created Quicken. Then, in a 1994 settlement in which Microsoft agreed not to compete

In the future we may wait a week or two before we decide to do something like this again. *(on the bid to by Intuit which was blocked by the Department of Justice)*

The quantum theory of gravity. *(the last thing you didn't understand)*

The flow of inside information will remain a critical issue for the antitrust investigators.
– *James Gleick*

I eat at McDonald's more than most people.

unfairly, they got you to promise to watch yourself for violations. You became your own enforcer. Now who really expected that to have any effect?

Things began to heat up even worse when Windows 95 was released. The DOJ filed a motion in federal court accusing Microsoft of violating the terms of your settlement. The issue at hand was your decision to integrate the Microsoft Internet browser, Explorer, into the new Windows 95 operating system. The argument headed back to the courts, where U.S. District Court Judge Thomas Jackson placed an injunction on Microsoft's release of Windows 95. He wanted you to release a version of Windows 95 that did not include Explorer.

This frustrated you unlike anything before. Your argument was that Explorer was fully integrated with Windows 95 and, if removed, Windows 95 would be nothing more than a block of useless, unrunable, code.

And while all this was going on, you and the Microsoft teams were quietly working away on the next generation: Windows 98, in which an updated version of Explorer was even more an integral part of the operating system. How were you to know that the DOJ wouldn't attack you on it, too? In a pre-emptive strike you invited a number of representatives of the computer industry to demonstrate their support of Microsoft in a May 5, 1998 press conference. In attendance were the CEOs of Compaq, CompUSA, Storm, and a professor of economics from Harvard. Other companies and groups signing their name to press release included: Dell, DEC, Eastman Kodak,

What's forbidden is for a company to use a monopoly in one area to try to secure a monopoly in a new and distinct market.
– Salon

Microsoft had proven time and time again that it would do anything to protect its operating systems business. Now, suddenly, the Internet was the battlefield.
– Edstrom & Eller

Everything Microsoft does ... is driven by the goal of giving consumers innovative tools and products that will improve their lives.

Microbasics Microjobs Microvisits Microvehicles Microhome
Microplay Microriches Micropolitics Microgiving Microfolk
Microreligion **Microworries** Microdreams Microimage Microman

97

Packard Bell, Staples, and the National Center for Disability Services. Participants declared that any delay in the release of Windows 98 to the marketplace would negatively impact the computer industry and the U.S. economy.

The show of support may have had an affect. On Tuesday, May 12, 1998, a U.S. Court of Appeals ruled that no action could be taken against Microsoft in its release of Windows 98. A sigh of relief, albeit brief, before the daily battle continued. On Thursday, May 14, the DOJ, in conjunction with twenty state attorneys, reluctantly agreed to defer the filing of a major antitrust suit against Microsoft in exchange for negotiations with Microsoft officals. Texas had recently backed out of the coalition after receiving letters from Dell and Compaq, who are housed in the Lone Star State.

You agreed to delay, for three days, shipping Windows 98 to computer stores and manufacturers. Talks went on through the weekend and after long hours of haggling, arguing, and plenty of coffee, the meeting ended, with everyone blaming everyone else, as is the way with such negotiations. Government officials were claiming that you had withdrawn a previously agreed-upon concession, and you wondered why anyone could expect you to include a competitor's software – in this case Netscape – in your product.

On Monday, May 18, 1998, after announcing that talks had broken down, the DOJ and their coalition of twenty states launched perhaps the largest antitrust lawsuit in U.S. history. Attorney General Janet Reno

The message I want a manager to communicate is, "I don't blame anybody in particular for this problem. What I care about is how well we rally around to come up with a new approach to resolve it."
(on mistakes)

We simply don't think the government should get involved in product design.

Computers are working for us so well that our economy has become totally dependent on them.

Microsoft does best when it has a successful competitor it can copy and then crush.
– *Edstrom & Eller*

In America, innovation is progress and progress means economic growth for the PC industry, for consumers, and for the nation. Windows 98 is important not only to Microsoft, but to the PC industry as a whole.

Playboy: Do the rumors bother you?

Microman: Rarely. But its difficult.

Forcing Microsoft to include Netscape's competing software in our operating system is like requiring Coca-Cola to include three cans of Pepsi in every six-pack it sells. *(on the DOJ's suggestion that you include Netscape in the release of Windows 98)*

commented on Microsoft's use of its "monopoly power" to gain a "chokehold" on Internet browsers. You could only shake your head: "We believe an antitrust lawsuit is counterproductive, costly to the taxpayers and ultimately will be unsuccessful in the courts." Then you started shipping Windows 98 to the stores. It had to be ready for release to the public by June 25, barely a month away.

But to make matters worse, the appeal on the injunction imposed in December of 1997 by Judge Jackson had yet to be completely resolved. The earlier judgement had cleared the way for Windows 98, but you and Microsoft weren't in the clear for what had happened with Windows 95. Until June 23, 1998, when a three-judge panel for the U.S. Court of Appeals gave you that clearance.

With the tiny exception of the major lawsuit by nearly half of America you were off to the races with all lanes clear. As for the tiny exception of the major lawsuit launched by nearly half of America, all you could say you said in an article in the *Wall Street Journal* titled: "We're Defending Our Right to Innovate."

PASTRY

As if losing time and money to software pirates and the U.S. government officials, lawyers, and politicians – every single one of them wearing eye patches behind closed doors – wasn't enough, now you've got to keep an eye out for projectiles. The greatest threat to you just may be a pie. Like the pie that hit you in the face while you were visiting Belgium in

Microbasics Microjobs Microvisits Microvehicles Microhome
Microplay Microriches Micropolitics Microgiving Microfolk
Microreligion **Microworries** Microdreams Microimage Microman

99

early February, 1998. Like some far-out comic book, the battle between Microman and Pieman is the stuff of legends.

MICROMAN VS. PIEMAN

by Hugues Henry [*bonjour@hugues.com*],Brussels.

So you want to be the one and only Microman! Be careful; just like The Joker has its nightmare, called Batman, you will have your own: Pieman! Pie, who? Forget Aron Kay, the Yippie activist who earned the title of Pieman for throwing pies in the faces of key figures from the Vietnam and the Watergate. Aron Kay retired in 1992 (even if he's on the Internet at the address http://www.pieman.org). Your own frightening Pieman is still working away. He has a lot of fans, a company of faithful activists. Any Microman candidate should know more about him:

Wednesday, 4th February 1998, Brussels, Belgium.
SPLASH! SPLASH! SPLASH! SPLASH!

"Four pies touched Bill Gates in the face." That's Him who speaks: your terrible Pieman, alias Le Gloupier, alias L'Entarteur ("he who pies" or "encaker" or "pie-er"), alias Noël Godin. How did Bill Gates react? "He had a kind of promotional smile that became a kind of smile made of sand," concluded Godin in his interview with the *Netly News* five days after the cream crime.

Godin: his first name "Noël" means "Christmas" in English (a real white Christmas with cream instead of snow). Godin is a 52-year-old Belgian author, film

I see us as an under-dog today, but I've seen us as an under-dog every day for the last twenty years.

In this business, by the time you realize you're in trouble, it's too late to save yourself.

Wasting somebody else's time strikes me as the height of rudeness.

I think that my looks were a disadvantage. *(on your youthful appearance during Microsoft's early days)*

historian, actor (*The Sexual Life of the Belgians*), and writer (*Cream and Punishment*). On Creamy Wednesday, the commando was armed to the teeth: "There were 25 pies in all. One of the secrets of the 'gloupinesque' operation is that you don't have to throw the

If you were Bill Gates, you would be curious about the pie-throwing incident. You would want to know who orchestrated the attack, where the intelligence on your schedule came from, and why, oh why, were you considered a target. You're just too clever to let something like that happen again.

Any software company that doesn't innovate won't be around long.

pies. You must put the pies point-blank in the face of the victim." And then? "The exhilaration of victory. Exquisite pleasure. The 'gloupinesque' operations have a 95 percent success rate. But each time we are stressed, and each time it's the same pleasure." His slogan: "Let's pie! Let's pie! Nincompoop guys!"

Who are you, Noël Godin? "I'm part of a gang of bad hellions that have declared the pie war on all the unpleasant celebrities in every kind of domain." And that war is a prolonged one: the French writer Marguerite Duras was the first victim, because "she represented for us the 'empty' novel," in November 1969 – nearly thirty years ago. "We began to act against 'empty' celebrities from the artistic world who where thinking they were the cat's whiskers. Then we attacked the TV news business in France, for instance, Patrick Poivre D'Arvor (a famous French TV presenter). Then it became political with Philippe Douste-Blazy in Cannes, the French minister of culture, or the other French minister Nicolas Sarkozy last year in Brussels."

We are acting to preserve competition and promote innovation in the computer software industry.
– *Attorney General Janet Reno*

Microbasics Microjobs Microvisits Microvehicles Microhome
Microplay Microriches Micropolitics Microgiving Microfolk
Microreligion **Microworries** Microdreams Microimage Microman

101

But why did you choose Bill Gates? "Because in a way he is the master of the world." Any Microman candidate knows that! "Then because he's offering his intelligence, his sharpened imagination and his power to the governments and to the world as it is today – that is to say gloomy, unjust and nauseating. He could have been a utopist, but he prefers being the lackey of the establishment. His power is effective and bigger than that of the leaders of the governments, who are only many-colored servants. So Bill Gates was at the top of our list of victims. The attack against him is symbolic. It's against hierarchical power itself."

Several months after the attack, Noël Godin hasn't changed his mind. In a way, he agrees on one point with the fans of Mr. MS: the one and only Microman is someone of importance! "Today I'm convinced that he really was the idyllic victim, more than I thought, more than the victims we are actually threatening, like Bill Clinton, Tony Blair or Jacques Chirac. They are puppets, only Gates is pulling the strings. Many people think that after him there is only one other powerful man in the world, the Pope." And the Belgian Pieman won't forget him in the future.

Let's try to be logical: if Bill Gates is the Master of the world, how was it possible for Pieman and his bad hellions to throw pies at him? Dear Microman, keep in my mind that the more power you have, the more you're alone: don't trust anybody, even your old friends. Pieman is proud to explain: "For several years, there's been a new phenomenon. Traitors appear in the entourage of our victims who contact

The lawsuit we filed today seeks to put an end to Microsoft's unlawful campaign to eliminate competition, deter innovation, and restrict consumer choice. In essence, what Microsoft has been doing, through a wide variety of illegal business practices, is leveraging its Windows operating system monopoly to force its other software products on consumers.

– *Assistant Attorney General Joel I. Klein, May 18, 1998*

us to give us first-hand information. Our victims, at first sight, are very unpleasant and they are far from being loved in their own circle; this is our trump. In the case of Bill Gates, a member of the staff of Microsoft Belgium contacted us and gave us a mysterious rendezvous. Thanks to him, the operation was a success. Of course we won't give his name. It's a secret; only a few know his identity. But we won't tell because we would be very amused if there was suspicion among the staff of Microsoft. 'Who's the traitor?!'"

Yes, Mr. Godin, who's the traitor? "He contacted us nine days before the attack. I saw him in a tavern and then he sent us several faxes with all the information we needed, until the last moment. Today he hasn't got any problem with Microsoft. No one has suspected him. He's not in trouble."

We repeat our question, Mr. Godin: who's the traitor? "This man told us he really loved Bill Gates in the past, saying that he was very cool and passionate. But little by little he considered that his power had tainted him, and that he was becoming more and more haughty with his own collaborators. So he considered – and he's not alone – that it wouldn't be bad to teach Bill a lesson, to bring him back to reality. That's how he explained to us why he was doing it. He's far from being a member of our band – he's not an anarchist and he likes his work with Microsoft – but he thought it had to happen."

One last time, Mr. Godin: who's the traitor? "Each week I receive three or four phone calls from strange people. At first sight, they are very kind, then they try

Microbasics Microjobs Microvisits Microvehicles Microhome
Microplay Microriches Micropolitics Microgiving Microfolk
Microreligion **Microworries** Microdreams Microimage Microman

103

to know more about this man from Microsoft, in a very clumsy way." What did the police do? Didn't Bill Gates pursue your commando? "No, it would be catastrophic for him and his reputation."

In the future, we fear it will be very hard for any Microman to travel the world without tasting one or more pies. But could Pieman attack Master Gates again? "We shall see. But we declare war on all the governments of the world, on Tony Blair, on Bill Clinton, on the Pope. For us, the Pope is a dangerous serial killer because he is against the preservative (birth control). On our blacklist, you will also find Demi Moore, alias *GI Jane*, and Tom Cruise and John Travolta, both followers of Scientology."

Is "Pieing" contagious? As contagious as Windows? There were thirty members of the Pieman's gang in the attack on Bill Gates. And it's just a beginning: "We have more and more sympathizers everywhere. We had thousands of propositions to help us, even abroad. We also have many enemies. But we are like the characters of a cartoon. We are like Laurel & Hardy, Bugs Bunny, the Marx Brothers, the Yippies of May 1968." No, Microman, not even money will stop them, nor encourage them, apparently. "We have never been pie mercenaries. But we've had several offers of a good amount of money. For instance, I had an offer to pie Catherine Deneuve in Cannes and also Sharon Stone. I refused. I love Catherine Deneuve and the movies of Jacques Demy; and that year Sharon Stone was in a western I really liked, *The Quick and the Dead*. So I had nothing against her. We are pie pirates. But if we receive money when we pie someone, we are not puri-

tan leftists. We received money once: in the case of (famous French singer and actor) Patrick Bruel. We offered the money to the anarchist Parisian magazine *Mordicus*. So if someone wants to give us money we won't misuse it. I could really enjoy life if I could earn much money doing this job! It's a big game and we have fun together. We want to live fast and to laugh as much as we can. We want to transform our lives just like Oscar Wilde wanted to. Everything is awful around us, so let's try to have fun."

· · • · ·

The ultimate question any Microman should ask to protect himself, finally, is very simple. It could be something like: "How can I contact Noël Godin?" Ready to smile? Embark your Explorer 4.0 and choose as the target the following URL: http://www.gloupgloup.com. There, you'll find some cream to eat. Believe us. And don't be too afraid of Noël Godin and his fellows; they won't try to kill you, but. . . . "We are comical terrorists and the pie is symbolic. The victim is only injured in his self-esteem. We take a lot of care that the pies can't hurt physically. The pastry is soft and full of cream." If you have the opportunity to go to Brussels, go the shop called Au Petit Pain Frais, chaussée de Haecht, and there you will taste the pie that splashed over the face of Bill Gates. Enjoy your meal, Microman!

ERROR: SYSTEM CRASH

Of course, you should also be worried about egg on your face. Be careful about mega-hyped product launches in front of thousands. When you demoed

Microbasics Microjobs Microvisits Microvehicles Microhome
Microplay Microriches Micropolitics Microgiving Microfolk
Microreligion **Microworries** Microdreams Microimage Microman

105

the new Windows 98 in April, 1998, at the Comdex Convention in Chicago there was a wee problem. While demonstrating how the new software will simplify the addition of hardware peripherals to a personal computer – in this case a scanner – the system crashed. Nothing but blue screen and error messages displayed to reporters, competitors, and computer lovers. A hapless employee who was running the demo as an expert could only exclaim, "Whoa!" Does he still have his job?

That must be why we're not shipping Windows 98 yet. *(on the crash of a demo during Comdex 1998)*

PRIVACY

The media were ready to photograph you with pie on your face. They were in attendance to see how you would respond to a major product crashing during a demo. And the media will be there to catch the next slip, too. Because with all the improvements in technology, they can keep as close an eye on you as you do on others.

[You know] as well as anyone that [your] days as technology king could come to a fairly swift end.
– *David Shenk*, The New Republic

People have been – will be – watching you closely. Floating their boats on Lake Washington past your new house, hoping to get a glimpse of you doing average, everyday things (do you garden?), whispering to each other as you walk through the airport terminal to get a fast-food burrito, even craning their necks driving down the freeway to see if that was you who just sped past them in the fast lane.

I'm worried about threats to privacy in the emerging electronic age.

And you and Melinda will have to be more careful about your late-night trysts in the glass-enclosed swimming pool. Anyone floating by on Lake Washington can see right into the pool, and you don't

Technology alone can't protect us.

As people really wake up to how much information about them is stored on computers and how it can be used, the issue of privacy – the balancing of individual liberties against the public's right to know – will be a hot topic.

want photographs showing up on the front pages of the tabloids.

Your popularity may not have reached rock-star proportions, but give it time. And realize that your life will, increasingly, become less your own everyday. It's not just Big Brother who is watching you.

Microdreams

Don't Look Back

At first, your dreams were simple and rather innocuous. You wanted to put a computer in every household, on every desk. Of course, you fully intended to be the software provider for each of those computers, so you'd do okay in the deal. The part of the dream that you made public didn't say anything about how much money you'd make by making sure that there was a computer on every desk.

It was kind of like a bonus.

These days it seems like you have dreams of world domination, but that is likely stretching the truth. You probably want to start with the United States. Worry about the rest when you come to it. But you have your work cut out for you. You still have over one hundred million people to equip with a computer. The nice thing is that they'll be setting up those computers with your programs.

Your vision for the future is the topic of your book,

In 1998 only forty percent of American households have personal computers. Less than half of these are connected to the Internet.

I think it's safe to say that within ten years the majority of all adults will be using electronic mail and living a form of Web lifestyle.

The Road Ahead. In it you describe your version of our upcoming world, and how it will be dominated by information. That information will be digital, you believe, which will allow everything everyone knows to be transformed, transmitted, and transplanted at increasing speeds. As far as you are concerned, we are witnessing the early development of the Information Highway. The moment at which we have only one cable wired into our homes – a cable providing all communication services – we will have entered the age of the Information Highway.

> People always overestimate how fast things will happen in the next two years, and underestimate what will happen in the next 10 years.

Television and computer screens will get thinner, portable computers will become smaller, and books will become tiny monitors that show text, pictures, audio, and video. Even our wallets and purses will become unnecessary, replaced by the wallet PC that you extoll. This device, in your future, will replace keys, theatre and airplane tickets, and money. Instead of carrying around all these cumbersome items, all any of us will need is our handy wallet PC. Credit cards, driver licenses, and library passes will all become antiquated artifacts in some museum. Even cold cash will be a thing of the past. Digital money will be the currency in the future you see.

> The information revolution is just beginning.

> I think of the wallet PC as the new Swiss Army knife.

All the information that we currently download from many sources will be digital, and will be easy to find using the many computer interfaces in our life. We will be able to search for specific details, filter out irrelevant information, and be notified when something of interest to us is announced. This will also mean that the information content will change. It will become much more specific, to appeal to specific interests.

Microbasics Microjobs Microvisits Microvehicles Microhome
Microplay Microriches Micropolitics Microgiving Microfolk
Microreligion Microworries **Microdreams** Microinage Microman

109

Entertainment – everything from movies to virtual reality to multimedia to games – will become more sophisticated and interactive. Businesses will become even more efficient, getting rid of paper altogether in favor of digital information. Contracts, memos, and application forms will be filled-out electronically. Information will be stored in a central location, accessible by everyone in an organization.

This doesn't mean the information will be free, but the cost of distributing it will be very small.

Buying and selling will become both simpler and more complicated. Buyers will be able to conduct research on products and comparison shop using electronic retailers. You foresee a day when the only people involved in a transaction are the buyer and the seller. So much for middlemen.

More than ever, an education that emphasizes general problem-solving skills will be important.

We are a long way off from having a completed highway. Fiber-optic cables will have to travel into every home, and new software will have to be written to help the new computers integrate seamlessly into our lives.

But don't worry about anyone accessing your personal, digital information. You are confident that encryption software will allow us to scramble our information so it can only be used by those we want to have it. For their eyes only.

As with all major changes, the benefits of the information society will carry costs.

And the best part of the advancing technology that seeps into every dimension of our lives is that it all, to some degree, needs an operating system. Every computer chip in every television, microwave, and bread-maker has a program that allows us to program them. You and Microsoft want to help all of these appliances work together by providing a Windows operating system that will be common for

We humans tend to anthropomorphize.

Tomorrow's communications systems will let you decide who can reach you in the morning, who can reach you at the dinner hour, and who can reach you at midnight. You'll set the rules.

We always focus on our own weaknesses. There's little benefit in spending time on what's going well.

Over the next few years, three-dimensional graphics will transform the face of popular computing.

A complete failure of the information highway is worth worrying about.

Until we are educating every kid in a fantastic way, until every inner city is cleaned up, there is no shortage of things to do.

every appliance, in every household. Your dreams have gone far beyond a simple computer on every desktop.

Not all of your dreams are so self-centred. You also have a vision for what you hope you are helping society to achieve. By donating money to education and by putting computers in libraries, you are at least making an effort at giving everyone the chance to benefit from the technology that made you, the technology that you hope will continue to make everyone's life better.

Microman and Paul Allen, 1982.

Microimage

A Public Persona

When you first became well-known – back in 1986 when Microsoft went public and you became an instant multi-millionaire – people saw you, thought of you as a visionary, a techno-radical.

Boy, how things have changed. You have realized the American dream almost too well, and people seem to resent that. You are David, grown into Goliath. In just over ten years your image has gone from being the boyish-looking computer nerd who was going to revolutionize computing and put a computer in every house, to a ruthless, power-hungry businessman who won't be satisfied until you own it all.

Talk about a backlash.

One of the reasons for this shift is that you are much more in the public eye now than ever before. In 1990, there were only a few articles being written about you, only a couple of interviews. Now everyone is scrambling to get an exclusive, wanting to know what you

[You are] the smartest guy I've ever met.
– *Steve Ballmer*

More impressive to some followers of the computer industry has been [your] ability to make the shift from creative genius to businessman, a transition other founders of high-tech-companies have failed to navigate.
– U.S. News & World Report, *July 21, 1986*

I think the fascination with wealth is always going to be there. It's unfortunate in that it creates a simplistic view of who I am and what I care about.

[You are] a postmodern P.T. Barnum.
– Mother Jones,
January/February 1998

I set a rule that people weren't allowed to send good news unless they sent around an equal amount of bad news to got with it.

[You aren't] just very rich and very famous … [you] embody an arresting social transformation.
– David Shenk, The New Republic

really think about the Internet, or how you live your life with Melinda and Jennifer. You are quiet about your personal life, keeping much of that to yourself, permitting only glimpses into Bill Gates, the husband, the dad, the guy-at-home-on-a-Sunday-afternoon.

Even as recently as 1995, you were reluctant to acknowledge or capitalize on your celebrity. And you are a celebrity, there is no escaping it now. Mentioned in the same breath as Bill Clinton, Madonna, and George Lucas. You use your celebrity to sell Microsoft, to sell software. But that celebrity also brings people with magnifying glasses and second-sight. They observe your every move, question your intent, assume the worst.

In *The New Republic*, David Shenk asks: "Does Gates really deserve this hostility, or is Microsoft-bashing just a cheap new common currency in an otherwise hyper-fragmented society?" In the end it doesn't really matter. You are under the microscope. You have ceased to be simply a computer geek who made good. You are now a cultural icon. You represent the world as it is today.

But to be fair, there are people out there who admire and support you. Sort of an anti-backlash faction. They revere you as they would any other person who is wealthy, powerful, and in the public eye. Does it make you nervous?

MICROMAN-SUPPORTIVE WEBSITES

www.stritch.edu/~bolem/gates.html · Bill Gates – The King!
www.teamgates.com · TeamGates.com
web.ns.s-chehire.ac.uk/~it

Microbasics Microjobs Microvisits Microvehicles Microhome Microplay Microriches Micropolitics Microgiving Microfolk Microreligion Microworries Microdreams **Microimage** Microman

113

MICROMAN IS LIKE. . .

The comparisons can't be denied. Your position in the United States and the world, in terms of wealth and power, have led to you being likened to historical figures such as Rockefeller, Carnegie, even Hearst.

Although John D. Rockefeller only had $1.4 billion at his richest moment, that equalled one-and-a-half percent of the United States' gross national product. Your $50 billion is only equal to six-tenths of one percent of today's gross national product. You're not the only one getting richer. So is the U.S.

Andrew Carnegie was the man who made his fortune – in steel – by the time he was thirty. The man who gave away most of his fortune promoting literacy and the arts. The man who built public libraries across America. You have pledged money and computers to connect those libraries to the Internet (Microsoft will donate software). It started at a ceremony in 1996 when you put computers into the Brooklyn Public Library's main branch. Now there is a foundation to coordinate the grants.

Newspaper baron William Randolph Hearst controlled, to a degree, how the ink spread on America's papers just as you decide, somewhat, what people will see on their computers. Hearst had his, at the time modern, extravagance in California, a vast estate overflowing with treasures collected from around the world. Your estate was designed by "ecology-friendly" architects to co-exist with nature and the elements in the Pacific Northwest. On the walls of your mansion, treasures of the

A century ago John D. Rockefeller gained control of the refinery business and oil pipelines, then leveraged that market power into control of oil production. So, in a way, is DOS a pipeline, and Microsoft owns it. – Forbes, *April 1, 1991*

Playboy: How do you define smart?

Microman: [Roll your eyes] It's an elusive concept . . . an ability to absorb new facts . . . to ask insightful questions . . . a capacity to remember.

Playboy: Are you smart?

Microman: By my own little definition I'm probably above average.

I have a natural instinct to hunt grim news. If it's out there, I want to hear it.

[You aren't] exactly a charismatic presence.
– Fortune, May 26, 1997

"We'd rather kill a competitor than grow the market?" Those are clear lies.

world will be displayed on wall screens.

The funny thing is, we don't really know what any of them were truly like. And, to be honest, we don't really know what you're like, either. The many interviews conducted with you in recent years only cloud your portrait. You hired a public relations firm to help you with public appearances – you no longer appear at interviews with tousled hair, wrinkled t-shirts, and dandruff flakes on your shoulders, but in suits and with a smile – but now we don't know whether you are the geeky computer nerd or the sociopathic businessman. We're confused.

In interviews you sound superior or modest, caustic or witty, brusque or gracious. It depends. You are always confident and self-assured.

CONSUMER CRUSADERS

Of course Ralph Nader – consumer rights activist – is against you. He writes columns with titles like: "The Microsoft Menace: Why I'm Leading a Crusade to Stop Its Drive for Cyberspace hegemony." He is organizing conferences to "debate the impact of Microsoft's business practices and to develop strategies to address the future of digital communications" ("While you're there, you can also register to meet other Microsoft bashers," Slate offers), and contributes to a web site called Appraising Microsoft. Ralph just wants to make sure that you don't run away with it all. He believes it is his job to make sure that the poor, unknowing public is protected.

Microbasics Microjobs Microvisits Microvehicles Microhome
Microplay Microriches Micropolitics Microgiving Microfolk
Microreligion Microworries Microdreams **Microimage** Microman

115

**WORDS USED TO
DESCRIBE YOU**

abrasive
adolescent
afraid
animated
arrogant
awkward
blasé
blunt
bore
boyish
brilliant
bullish
bully
calm
cheater
childlike
cocky
cool
competitive
condescending
confident
cynical
Darwinian
dishonest
dropout
driven
eccentric
enthusiastic
fear
feisty
friendly
gangly
geek
greedy
hungry

I know what you're thinking to yourself: "There's always something to rage against, isn't there, Ralph?"

MICROMAN: THE CARTOON

In an episode of the Fox Network's 1997-1998 season of *The Simpsons*, Homer decides to moonlight by starting a business that operates over the Internet. He becomes "The Internet King."

Dreaming of the fortune he will make, Homer reads *Internet for Dummies: Remedial Edition* (musing, "Oh, they have the Internet on computer now"), and he is paid a visit by a character called "Bill Gates." Gates is joined by two stereotypical nerds, both wearing black, horn-rimmed glasses: a skinny guy in too-short pants, a short-sleeved dress shirt complete with pocket protector, and an overweight guy with a crew cut.

The Gates character explains that he wants to buy Homer's company. Homer, thinking his ship has come in, accepts, and is

And when Microsoft asks to license your technology, you may not always find it easy to say no.

— James Gleick

shocked when the two nerds accompanying the Gates character start wrecking everything in sight. The Gates character laughs maniacally, explaining, "I didn't get rich by writing a lot of cheques."

If you were Bill Gates you might not be happy about this portrayal. You may even have had lawyers contact the Fox network to ensure that the episode was never rebroadcast. To what lengths would you go? Are you ready and willing to take the elbow jabs that come with success, fame, and fortune?

Today the perception of Microsoft as the evil empire is greater than ever, measured in personal attacks on [you] from rival computer moguls, and on the internet, the collective unconscious of computerdom.

– New York Times, November 28, 1996

influential
insatiable
intense
juvenile
keen
kid-like
knowledgeable
liar
megalomaniacal
monomaniacal
methodical
modest
neutral
overt
paranoid
passionate
patient
placid
powerful
predatory
quick
quick-tempered
razor-sharp
relentless
rich
ruthless
self-assured
self-confident
smart
superior
tenacious
tireless
unkempt
unfazed
vehement
vindictive
witty
youthful

Microbasics Microjobs Microvisits Microvehicles Microhome
Microplay Microriches Micropolitics Microgiving Microfolk
Microreligion Microworries Microdreams **Microimage** Microman

117

MICROMAN: THE DEVIL

According to some, you might be the Devil incarnate. Invoking Revelation 13:18 ("Here is wisdom. Let him who has understanding calculate the number of the beast, for it is the number of a man: His number is 666."), and numerology, the logic is simple:

You are the third Bill Gates of your family. Bill Gates 3. First, convert the letters of your name to the ASCII-values used by computers.

B (66), I (73), L (76), L (76), G (71), A (65), T (84), E (69), S (83), 3 (3). Now, sum the numbers associated with the letters of your name:

TOTAL = 666

I think this is a wonderful time to be alive. *(1995)*

But there's more. . . .

Again invoking Revelations (13:16 states: "He causes all, both small and great, rich and poor, free and slave, to receive a mark on their right hand or on their foreheads." Further, in 13:18 it is written: ". . . no one may buy or sell except one who has the mark or the name of the beast, or the number of his name."), web-bound soothsayers suggest that "Windows compatible" may be the dreaded name.

source: Greenspun, Philip. Why Bill Gates is Richer Than You

Microman

Who Are You Now?

So there you have it. Everything you need to know about what it takes to be a Microman or Microwoman. Opinions and beliefs, actions and behaviors, lifestyle and belongings.

I have lots of things to be thankful for, not the least of which are eyeglasses.

You surround yourself with intelligent people. You have friends and un-friends and even a few enemies. Which group a person falls into depends, in whole or in part, on whether you have done business with them and if you have, how satisfied they were with the deal.

You may not always be comfortable in social situations – but you're learning. You now understand the importance of a public image, and have worked hard to construct and maintain the picture you want people to have of you.

You immerse yourself in technology: microprocessors, video screens, keyboards, communication links, software. The things that got you where you are today will lead you to tomorrow. And you're

Right now I don't want to be huger. I'm huger than I want to be. I'd like to shrink a little. (on your celebrity status)

Fiction is true randomness.

I'd say that my job, throughout all this, has been, I think, the most fun job I can imagine having.

I'm still thrilled by the feeling that I'm squinting into the future and catching that first revealing hint of revolutionary possibilities.

taking everyone else with you.

You own stuff: cars, houses, companies. What you'd like to have, you purchase. Things you want to be a part of, you integrate.

You are fiercely determined. Driven. Racing toward an undetermined future that the world has – however inadvertently – asked you to prophesy and fulfill. You confront and resolve threats by imposing your will to be successful, to achieve. To win.

And you are in the privileged position of being able to use your seemingly unlimited resources to turn events to their favor.

Remember, though, that life is not all wine and roses. For every crest you surf is a sandbar to crash into. Prepare yourself for the inevitable downturn. Moments like these make you stronger, help to form who you are.

Bill appears to lead a charmed life. Fortune has smiled upon him. This makes your task more difficult. A challenge. Becoming Micromen and Microwomen will not be easy. But it will be rewarding. Steel yourselves to the task.

Good luck. And above all, don't forget who helped you along the way.

**MICROMAN:
PERSONAL DETAILS**

ROLE MODELS
Napoleon, Albert Ein-
stein, Leonardo da
Vinci.

FAVORITE BOOKS
The Catcher in the Rye
(J.D. Salinger), *The
Great Gatsby* (F. Scott
Fitzgerald), *A Sepa-
rate Peace* (John
Knowles).

FAVORITE AUTHORS
Philip Roth, John
Irving, Ernest J.
Gaines, Donald
Knuth, David
Halberstam.

FAVORITE SINGER
Frank Sinatra.

FAVORITE CARTOONS
*Ren & Stimpy,
Rugrats.*

**FAVORITE
PUBLICATIONS**
*The Economist, The
Wall Street Journal,
Business Week, Time,
USA Today.*

I consider failure on a
regular basis.

Bibliography

BOOKS

Adney, Tappan. *The Klondike Stampede*. Vancouver, BC: UBC
Press, 1899.

Carlton, Jim. *Apple: The Inside Story of Intrigue, Egomania, and
Business Blunders*. New York: Random House, 1997.

Edstrom, Jennifer and Marlin Eller. *Barbarians Led by Bill Gates:
Microsoft From the Inside: How the World's Richest Corporation Wields Its Power*. New York: Henry Holt, 1998.

Gates, Bill, Nathan Myhrvold and Peter Rinearson. *The Road
Ahead*. New York: Penguin, 1995.

Martinsen, Ella Lung. *Black Sand and Gold: True Alaska-Yukon
Gold-Rush Story*. Portland, OR: Binford & Mort, 1956.

PERIODICALS

"America's Most Admired Companies." *Fortune*, March 2, 1998
(vol. 137, iss. 4).

Arenson, Karen W. "Gates of Microsoft Gives $15 Million to Har-
vard." *New York Times* (October 30, 1996).

"Best Companies to Work For in America." *Fortune*, January 12, 1998 (vol. 137, iss. 1).

Daglish, Brenda. "Genius at Work: He is the Richest Man in America, But Can William Gates Stay on Top of the Heap?" *Maclean's* (Monday, May 11, 1992).

Dobbyn, Tim. "U.S. Files Major Antitrust Case vs Microsoft." *Reuters* (May 18, 1998).

Egan, Timothy. "Houses by Gates: Virtual and Real; It Takes Time to Build Xanadu." *New York Times* (January 12, 1995).

"The 400 Richest Americans." *Forbes*, October 21, 1986 (vol. 138, iss. 9).

"The 400 Richest Americans." *Forbes*, October 13, 1997 (vol. 160, iss. 8).

Gabriel, Trip. "Catching Up With: Bill Gates; Filling Potholes in 'Road Ahead.'" *New York Times* (November 28, 1996).

Gates, Bill. "Inside 'The House.'" *Newsweek*, vol. 126, no. 2 (November 27, 1995).

Gates, Bill. "U.S. v. Microsoft: We're Defending Our Right to Innovate." *The Wall Street Journal* (May 20, 1998).

Gleick, James. "Making Microsoft Safe for Capitalism." *New York Times Magazine* (November 5, 1995).

Goldberg, Carey. "What's Wrong With This Picture?" *New York Times* (May 18, 1997).

Hirsh, Michael. "The Feds' Case Against Bill Gates." *Newsweek*, vol. 131, no. 10 (March 9, 1998.

Isaacson, Walter. "The Gates Operating System." *Time*, vol. 149, no. 2 (January 13, 1997).

Johnson, Kirk. "Support for Rural and Inner-City Libraries." *New York Times* (October 9, 1996).

Johnston, David Cay. "Warning: These Numbers May Depress You." *New York Times* (July 20, 1997).

Kennedy, John. "Interview With Bill Gates." *George*, vol. 2, no. 2 (February, 1997).

Kirkpatrick, David. "He Wants *All* Your Business-And He's Starting to Get It." *Fortune*, vol. 135, no. 10 (May 26, 1997).

Lewis, Michael. "The Capitalist; What Will Gates Give?" *New York Times* (October 13, 1996).

Levy, Steven. "Bill's New Vision." *Newsweek*, vol. 126, no. 22 (November 27, 1995).

Levy, Steven. "Microsoft vs. The World." *Newsweek*, vol. 131, no. 10 (March 9, 1998).

Microbasics Microjobs Microvisits Microvehicles Microhome
Microplay Microriches Micropolitics Microgiving Microfolk
Microreligion Microworries Microdreams Microimage Microman

125

Levy, Steven and Mark Whitaker. "Software is My Life."
Newsweek, vol. 126, no. 2 (November 27, 1995).

The London Observer (published in *The Montreal Gazette*,
Wednesday, July 12, 1995).

"Most Generous Americans." *Fortune*, February 2, 1998 (vol. 137, iss. 2).

"100 Super-Rich Owners of American Business." *U.S. News &
World Report*, July 21, 1986 (vol. 101, iss 3).

Rensin, David. "The Bill Gates Interview." *Playboy* (December,
1994).

Schlender, Brent. "On the Road With *Chairman Bill.*" *Fortune*, vol
135, no. 10 (May 26, 1997).

Shenk, David. "Slamming Gates." *The New Republic*, vol. 218, no. 4
(January 26, 1998).

Silverstein, Ken. "The Microsoft Network." *Mother Jones*, vol. 23,
no. 1 (January/February 1998).

Wiegner, Kathleen K. and Julie Pitta. "Can anyone stop Bill
Gates?" *Forbes*, vol. 147, no.7 (April 1, 1991).

Zachary, G. Pascal. "His Way." *Mother Jones*, vol. 23, no. 1 (Janu-
ary/February 1998).

AUDIO & VIDEO

Allison, David. *Bill Gates Interview*. Transcript of Video History
Archive, Smithsonian Institution: National Museum of American History, December 1993.

"Bill Gates Addresses America's Newspaper Publishers." Transcript
of Key Note Address, *E&P Interactive*. Chicago: Newspaper Association of America Publisher's Convention (April 29, 1997).

WEBSITE PUBLICATIONS

Brandt, Richard and Eric Nee. "Bill Gates: An Interview." Online.
Internet. *Upside Magazine* (April, 1996). Available http://
www.upside.com/.

Crockett, Barton. "Microsoft Wins Appeals Court Ruling on Windows 98." *MSNBC* (May 12, 1998). Online. Internet. Available
http://www.msnbc.com/news/default.asp.

"Gates: From OS to Internet." PC Week Staff. *PC Week Online*, May 30, 1996. Online. Internet. Available http://www.zdnet.com/pcweek/.

Halton, David. "Microsoft Starts Shipments Despite Lawsuits." *cbc.ca* (May 18, 1998). Online. Internet. Available http://cbc.ca/.

"Inside Bill's Gates." *U.S. News & World Report Online*, December 1, 1997. Online. Internet. Available http://www.usnews.com/usnews/home.htm.

Nader, Ralph. "The Microsoft Menace: Why I'm Leading a Crusade to Stop Its Drive for Cyberspace Hegemony." *Slate* (October 29, 1997). Online. Internet. Available http://www.slate.com/toc/FrontPorch.asp.

"Outlook." *U.S. News & World Report Online*, July 7, 1997. Online. Internet. Available http://www.usnews.com/usnews/home.htm.

Rosenberg, Scott. "The Browser War Goes Thermonuclear." *Salon*, (May 20, 1998). Online. Internet. Available http://www.salon.com/.

"Why Bill Gates and Steve Jobs Made Up." *U.S. News & World Report Online*, August 18, 1997. Online. Internet. Available http://www.usnews.com/usnews/home.htm.

Williams, Pete. "Justice Unlikely to Delay Windows 98." *MSNBC* (May 11, 1998). Online. Internet. Available http://www.msnbc.com/news/default.asp.

Credits

Adney, Tappan. *The Klondike Stampede*. Vancouver, BC: UBC Press, 1899: p.315.

Gleick, James. "Making Microsoft Safe for Capitalism." *New York Times Magazine* (November 5, 1995).

Greenspun, Philip. *Bill Gates Personal Wealth Clock*. http://www.webho.com/WealthClock

Greenspun, Philip. *Why Bill Gates Is Richer Than You*.

http://photo.net/philg/humor/bill-gates.html

Marcus, Evan. *Bill Gates Net Worth Page.* http://www.quuxu-um.org/~evan/bgnw.html

Martinsen, Ella Lung. *Black Sand and Gold: True Alaska-Yukon Gold-Rush Story.* Portland, OR: Binford & Mort, 1956: pp. 127-129, 160-162.

Templeton, Brad. *Bill Gates Wealth Index.* http://www.temple-tons.com/brad/billg.html

PHOTOS

page 6: Reuters/Lou Dematteis/Archive Photos
page 10: *Seattle Post-Intelligencer*
page 14: *Seattle Post-Intelligencer*
page 18: *Seattle Post-Intelligencer*
page 20: *Seattle Post-Intelligencer*
page 30: Tom Reese/*Seattle Times*
page 40: AP Photo
page 44: Bob O'Rear/ *Seattle Post-Intelligencer*
page 48: Steve Ringman/*Seattle Times*
page 54: Mike Siegel/*Seattle Times*
page 66: AP Photo
page 70: B. Weil/*Toronto Star*
page 90: AP Photo
page 106: *Seattle Post-Intelligencer*
page 110: Barry Wong/*Seattle Times*
page 118: *Seattle Post-Intelligencer*
page 122: *Seattle Post-Intelligencer*